PRAISE

The Leader In the Mirror

"Reading The Leader In the Mirror will take the reader only a few hours. Applying the lessons in it will take a lifetime."

Raymond Arroyo
Chief Diversity Officer
Aetna

"Ted's back and none too soon! This is the perfect sequel to The Leader's Lobotomy. The leadership journey is one of continuous improvement and discovery. As leaders we are often taught to keep our vision on the horizon, however, if we are going to be the best leaders we can be we must look in the mirror and take inventory of our skills and work on a continuous plan for improvement. This book provides us a simple and common sense way of doing that. "

Thomas J. Sullivan
President & Chief Executive Officer
Symmetry Medical Inc.

"Practical, simple, entertaining, and powerful."

Eric Guerin
VP Finance
Novartis

"The work of leadership is our life's work and this book is a wonderful, engaging tool to help guide that journey. A must have for the learning leader's tool box."

Kaye Foster-Cheek
SVP Global Human Resources
Onyx Pharmaceuticals

The Leader In The Mirror

The Legacy Leader's Critical Self Assessment

Anthony Lopez

Also in this volume:

The Leader's Lobotomy: *The Legacy Leader Avoids Promotion-Induced Amnesia*

A Fable

authorHOUSE®

AuthorHouse™
1663 Liberty Drive
Bloomington, IN 47403
www.authorhouse.com
Phone: 1-800-839-8640

First published by AuthorHouse   11/28/2011

ISBN: 978-1-4670-2703-8 (sc)
ISBN: 978-1-4670-2702-1 (hc)
ISBN: 978-1-4670-2701-4 (e)

Library of Congress Control Number: 2011917118
Printed in the United States of America

Anthony B. López
5580 Camino DeBryantYorba Linda,
CA, 92887260-341-9737
ablopez85@yahoo.com
www.thelegacyleader.net
Other books by Anthony López
"The Legacy Leader:
Leadership With a Purpose"
ISBN: 1-4107-3936-8
"Breakthrough Thinking:
The Legacy Leader's Role in Driving Innovation"
ISBN: 1-4208-3496-7

"The Leader's Lobotomy:
The Legacy Leader Avoids Promotion-Induced Amnesia"
ISBN: 978-1-4398-1150-2
"See You at the Wake:
Healing Relationships Before It's Too
Late"ISBN: 1-4184-1127-2
"The Legacy Leader: 2ⁿᵈ Edition"
ISBN: 978-1-61663-614-2
"Jag: Christian Lessons From My Golden Retriever"
ISBN: 978-4670-2694-9

DEDICATION

For Yvette. I love you.

Contents

FOREWORD

Many people consider leadership an art form; other experts think of it as a science. Some look at leadership as a set of processes and methodologies aimed at driving certain outcomes from a group of people. However, no matter what school of leadership thought you ascribe to, there can be little argument that leadership can be taught, and that with practice, individuals can indeed become better leaders.

Thinking back on the books that have impacted me the most, I realize that they all had lessons that were easy to apply in real life. *The Legacy Leader Series of Books* has that inherent quality to it. In the first three books of the series, *The Legacy Leader, Breakthrough Thinking* and *The Leader's Lobotomy*, Tony captured the essence of leadership, the fundamental principles and mechanics of leadership, and provided us a clear pathway to becoming more effective leaders. In *The Leader In the Mirror* he guides us through what is arguably the most important step in our leadership journey: a critical self-assessment.

Each leader's journey is unique and personal. There are countless factors that can impact our growth and development as leaders; factors such as the formal and informal education we are exposed to, our life experiences, the mentoring and coaching we receive along the way, the failures and successes we experience, and maybe even a bit of luck. Regardless of what stage of our life journey we find ourselves in – whether it's early in our careers or at the twilight of a lifetime of successful leadership – there is always something that we can learn and improve on to become more effective. Perhaps more importantly, what we learn today will ensure that we will be even better tomorrow. Thus, leaders must be willing to do a critical self-assessment of their skills. There are many methods available to do an individual assessment. However, can any method be more effective and laser-focused than a brutally honest and critical self-evaluation? Who knows us better than ourselves? Who is in a better position or has better insight into what our individual strengths and weaknesses are than ourselves?

This does not mean that we can't or shouldn't seek help or solicit feedback when conducting a self-assessment. The ownership of our personal assessment, however, rests with each of us. In the end, if we can't be honest with ourselves, hearing someone else's opinion of us will have little or no impact.

Tony brings his personal leadership experience of over twenty five years to his writing. Since they're based upon experience, the concepts and ideas presented in this book work! They work best for those individuals with a healthy sense of self-awareness and emotional intelligence who will be able to maximize this next step in their leadership journey. This book will benefit those who are willing to take that sometimes difficult look in the mirror, create an action plan, and actually make changes in their attitudes and behaviors to improve who they are as leaders. The process of conducting a self-assessment is an ongoing one; it's not a one time deal. We must all be in a continuous state of learning and growing. Thus, *The Leader In the Mirror* is not the kind of book you read once and forget about a week later. It's the kind of book that you keep handy on your desk and refer to often as you challenge yourself to become a better leader tomorrow than you are today.

Robert Rodriguez, PhD

Director – Kaplan Center for Corporate Learning

Kaplan University

Author of "Latino Talent: Effective Strategies to Recruit, Retain & Develop Hispanic Professionals" (Wiley, 2008).

Dr. Robert Rodriguez is a leading expert on Latino diversity in corporate America. His book, *"Latino Talent"* (www.latinotalentbook.com) is used by numerous corporations looking to more effectively tap into the Latino talent pool. He serves on the board of directors for the National Forum of Latino Healthcare Executives (NFLHE) and is the former board chair for Hispanic Alliance for Career Enhancement (HACE). Robert is also a member of PRIMER, a network of Latino business and professionals. Dr. Rodriguez has won numerous awards including being named as one of the top emerging stars age 40 and under in *Latino Leaders Magazine* in 2009, the Hispanic Heroes award and a Rising Latino Stars award by the Hispanic Chamber of Commerce. He received his doctorate in Organization Development and is a graduate of the Latino Leadership Institute at UCLA.

INTRODUCTION

The leader's journey is one of exploration, growth and self- discovery. That has certainly been the case for me. Over the past twenty five years, I have studied the subject of leadership and have come to the conclusion that it's an evolutionary process.

Biologists define evolution as the change in genetic material of a population of organisms from one generation to the next. Although the changes in any one generation may be small, differences accumulate with each passing generation. Over time, these changes become more evident and significant. In fact, sometimes this slow transformation is even the genesis of a new species.

The basis of evolution is that genes are passed from one generation to the next. These genes give organisms their inherited traits. Mutations of these traits begin to take place as the environment changes, or as the need develops for the organisms to adapt and survive.

I don't blindly ascribe to Darwin's theory of evolution. As a Christian, I know that God created man, the universe and everything in it. Whether He chose to use the evolutionary process or not, I do not pretend to know. I will leave that debate to the greater thinking minds of our time. However, as it relates to the leadership process, a theory of evolution makes sense to me.

According to Darwin's theory, evolution is a slow, gradual process. In *On the Origin of Species,* which was published in 1858, Darwin wrote:

> *...natural selection acts only by taking advantage of slight successive*

variations; she can never take a great and sudden leap, but must advance by short and sure, though slow steps.

Darwin concludes that it is this natural selection that leads to survival of the strongest members of a species.

The same is true with leadership – not only in our own personal leadership journey as individuals, but also in the evolution of the science of leadership. Over time, with new insights, ideas and even new technologies, leaders evolve and change. Hopefully, from one generation of leaders to the next, we pass down the best "genes" and leaders get better with every passing age. Unfortunately, that's not always the case, but the journey continues and our quest to become better leaders must go on. Importantly, our mandate to create an even better generation of leaders for the future also goes on.

This is the fifth book in *The Legacy Leader Series*. The first – *The Legacy Leader: Leadership With a Purpose* – began with my thesis that, of all the traits a leader can and must posses, only two are non-negotiable. Those two non-negotiable qualities are character and integrity. All other qualities and skills necessary for effective leadership can be acquired via education, experience, and especially The School of Hard Knocks. Character and integrity, however, are woven into the very fabric of our DNA and are non-negotiable.

Once character and integrity are compromised, the leader fails to reach the maximum level of effectiveness they could have attained had their character and integrity remained whole. *The Legacy Leader* also addressed the mechanics of leadership. It presented the most fundamental qualities and behaviors that leaders must exhibit if they are to build "Achieving Organizations" and a personal legacy of which they can be proud.

The second book in *The Legacy Leader Series* is *Breakthrough Thinking: The Legacy Leader's Role in Driving Innovation*. It addressed what the Legacy Leader must do to drive teams and organizations to accomplish things they might have initially thought impossible.

In the third volume, *The Leader's Lobotomy*, we explore what can happen to high level leaders who, suddenly and without warning, develop a horrible disease called PIA – Promotion-Induced Amnesia. In this humorous fictional account, we address a subject of profound significance: the leader's need to ensure that they practice the most fundamental and important elements of leadership. We introduced the main characters of Jim, a recently promoted executive, and Ted, his Corporate Guardian Angel. The story walked us through a year in Jim's life as a new executive, and how Ted coached him on important leadership fundamentals to ensure that Jim avoided contracting the dreaded Promotion-Induced Amnesia. The 2nd Edition of *The Leader's Lobotomy* is included in this book as Section II.

The Leader In the Mirror picks up the action eight years later when Jim is promoted to president of his company. Ted – back by popular demand – re-enters Jim's life to help him take a hard look in the mirror and conduct an honest leadership self-assessment, and to encourage him to stick with the process even if he doesn't like what he sees.

As in *The Leader's Lobotomy*, any similarities between characters in this short story and individuals you know – including yourself – are not a coincidence, and are very much on purpose. Although the story is fictional, many of you will relate to its universal truths. I know I do. I admit that the tale feels somewhat autobiographical at times. I've looked in the leader's self-assessment mirror, and the reflection is not always pretty. However, taking that critical step of self-assessment is a must for any leader who wants to become a true Legacy Leader and be the best they can be.

As I pen this book, I am humbled by the realization of the significant gaps in my own leadership abilities. If failure is a great teacher, then I am learning much along the way! One thing I do know for sure: the moment you become complacent and start believing that you have reached the peak in your leadership game is the moment when you have the greatest opportunity to fail. Thus, as it was with my previous books, I write this one with myself as the target audience. Despite some setbacks and encouraged by a few successes along my leadership journey, I am committed and striving to become a Legacy Leader. I have a long way yet to go.

Shall we make the trip together?

Anthony López

SECTION ONE

The Leader In the Mirror

PREFACE

From Chapter 1

Of

The Leader's Lobotomy

A Fable

The Legacy Leader Avoids

Promotion-Induced Amnesia

Jim was feeling very good about himself. He had an extra spring in his step as he made his way to his car in the parking lot of ITA, Inc. Jim had been an ITA employee for more than fifteen years, working his way up from third shift production supervisor to his most recent position as Director for U.S. Operations. He waved to a few co-workers as they entered the building to begin work on the second shift. He realized that it had been a while since he had been on the shop floor to visit the production folks on the second and third shifts. He made a mental note to do that later in the week.

He had made that mental note before.

"Hey Jim, hold up!" called Maryann as she rushed to catch up with him. Maryann was Worldwide Director of Quality Control.

"Hi, Maryann. How are you?"

"Just fine, thanks. But not as good as you," she replied with a sincere smile. "I just want to say congratulations!"

Jim shook Maryann's outstretched hand. "Thanks Maryann. I didn't think the announcement had been made yet."

"Oh it hasn't," she winked. "But, you know, I've got a few connections around here."

Jim knew that was an understatement. Maryann was more well-connected than a light bulb. She knew everything happening at ITA before anybody else.

"You are going to be a fantastic Vice President for World Wide Operations," she said.

Jim liked the way that sounded. He could not hide his pride. "Thank you, Maryann. I am really excited about this."

"You earned it," she said.

"Well, you helped me get there, that's for sure." Jim meant what he said. Maryann had been with the company for more than twenty five years, and on Jim's first day at ITA she took him under her wing and had mentored him ever since. She had been a wise and caring advisor to him over the years.

A smart, charismatic, and attractive middle-aged woman, Maryann was respected by all, admired by most, and disliked by only a few. One thing was certain – she knew her stuff, and she breathed and lived ITA's business. In Jim's mind, she was a strong and driven leader. Maryann had never made it to the executive ranks, but it wasn't for lack of skill or ability. It was a matter of personal choice. She never wanted it.

"Now the hard work begins, Jim," Maryann warned. "Whatever you do, promise me you will not forget the lessons you've learned along the way."

Jim looked puzzled.

"Maryann!" called a voice from the second floor window. "You have an urgent call from the Lyon office."

"Ahhrr," she said with mock frustration. "The French! Will they never leave me alone? Got to run; see you in the morning, Mr. VP."

"Okay. See you in the morning."

Jim started to walk toward the parking lot again, but suddenly turned back and shouted out to Maryann just as she was about to enter the building.

"Hey, Maryann! What lessons are you talking about?"

"All of them!" she replied without missing a step. She disappeared into the building.

Jim stood frozen for a moment. *What did Maryann mean by that?*

"Hey Jim," Perry said as he zoomed by on his bicycle.

Jim snapped back to reality. "Oh, hey Perry," he said absently. He continued his walk toward the car. It was parked in the south lot, affectionately known as the "Loser's Lot." Jim smiled at the realization that this was one of the last times he would have to park back there. The VP title carried with it a larger office with a view of the small, picturesque lake on ITA's property, a much larger salary, a staff of eight directors, and a coveted parking spot close to the building's main entrance.

He finally made it to his car before he realized just how hot it was that day. Jim opened the car door, and a rush of superheated air from inside his Acura TL hit his face. He winced.

––––––––––

"Hello?" Jim said into his cell phone.

"Are you on your way home?"

Jim recognized the sweet voice of his bride of ten years, Marisol. "Yes, I just left the office, and I'll be home in about thirty minutes or so."

"I made reservations at Torrence. They are chilling the champagne," Marisol said with a hint of flirting in her voice. "And I am wearing something spectacular."

Jim grinned. "I am sure you will look incredible." That was nothing if not the truth. Marisol was a beautiful and sophisticated woman. A labor law

5

attorney by day and a cycling fanatic by night, she enjoyed her long quiet rides in the evening, when the sun was not too hot and the days lasted until almost nine thirty. "I guess I have to dress up also?"

"Of course," Marisol demanded. "I already picked out a suit for you."

"I have to wear a suit?" Jim hated wearing suits.

"Yes, a suit. We are going to a show after dinner, and Keith and Tina will be joining us for the show."

"Keith and Tina are coming with us?" Jim asked. Keith Lawrence had been the president of ITA for about three years, and he and Jim had become good friends. Marisol and Tina were as close as sisters.

"Surprise!" she said, proud of herself for keeping the secret for over a week. She knew about his promotion before he did! "Now, hurry home."

As he hung up the phone, in his mind he could smell the sweet perfume that his wife usually wore. He was so proud of that woman! The daughter of immigrant parents, Marisol had arrived in the United States at age thirteen, unable to speak more than a few words in English.

She had a work ethic and a passion for life like no one else Jim had ever met. Fiercely competitive, self-driven and motivated, she ultimately rose to the top of her high school class, graduating number one and earning academic scholarships to every school she applied to.

Most amazing to Jim was how she had mastered English. She was now fluent in both her native Spanish and English, which she spoke with out a hint of an accent. Along the way she had also learned Italian and a bit of French. Now, she worked tirelessly to promote labor laws to improve corporate efficiencies while protecting the rights of all employees. Jim genuinely admired his wife.

————————

Traffic was unusually heavy for this early in the afternoon. The two-lane highway that took Jim home each day passed a few small towns, and there always seemed to be a bit of a slow down as drivers watched out for local cops.

Jim's mind was not on his driving. He was deep in thought about his new position. He had worked so hard toward this. He was bypassed for the position a few years earlier and almost made the mistake of leaving the company then. Maryann had talked him into staying. Somehow she had managed to tell Jim that he was not ready for the position without making him feel bad about it. Now as he looked back, he realized that she had been right. He had needed a few more years to grow as a leader before tackling the enormous challenge now ahead of him.

"Bet you think your poop don't stink now, huh?"

The deep voice with a strong New York City accent almost scared Jim out of his seat belt. He yelled as he looked to his right to find a strange man sitting in the passenger seat.

"Who the heck are you? And how did you get in my car?" Jim asked startled, his eyes wide open.

"I'm Ted," the man said as he stuck a huge cigar in his mouth and puffed on it. It was lit, but there was no smoke. "I just sorta appeared, you know what I mean?"

"No, I don't know what you mean," Jim replied, half scared and half angry. "You better get out of my car right now or you are going to be in big trouble." Jim had no idea what trouble he was referring to, but he was trying to hide his fear by sounding tough.

The driver in the car behind Jim's leaned on his horn impatiently at Jim's inaction after the red light had been green for more than five seconds.

"Green means go," the cigar smoking man said.

"I am not moving this car until you get out. I mean it, get out!"

"Relax, Jim Givens of 13244 Westward Drive. You are thirty-nine years of age, married ten years to the former Marisol Butero, thirty-five – and a gorgeous woman by the way – you have no children, you have a Labrador retriever, you have a bachelor's degree in mechanical engineering, an MBA from Duke, played high school and college baseball. You like to fish and play soccer. You prefer red wine, although Marisol is a white wine type, which makes it tough at restaurants sometimes." The man was rattling off the details in a rapid monotone, as if he were playing them back from a recorder. "Shall I continue?"

"Look mister, I don't know who you are or how you know so much about me, but I'm calling the police." Jim reached for his cell phone and dialed 9-1-1.

"Your phone has no signal," Ted said confidently.

Jim looked at the screen on his phone. He saw four bars, indicating a strong signal. "Guess you don't know everything after all," he said as he brought the phone back to his ear.

"Look again," Ted ordered.

His phone was dead.

"Okay, what do you want?"

By now there were a dozen cars behind him, beeping their horns in frustration. "You can start by getting out of the way before you become a victim of road rage."

Jim, unsure of what else to do, stepped gently on the gas and began moving forward. "So, are you going to tell me who you are?"

"I told you, my name is Ted. I am your CGA," Ted replied sarcastically.

"CGA? What's that?"

"Corporate Guardian Angel," Ted said with disgust. He shook his head. "Boy, is that stupid. That is such a dumb title. You think they could come up with a better acronym."

"You are my Corporate Guardian Angel? Is this a new program instituted by ITA?" Jim asked, trying to make sense of this strange man who appeared out of thin air and was now sitting in his car.

"Nope, it's nothing like that. Just a silly program started about five years ago when someone upstairs decided that too many leaders were acting as if they had gotten lobotomies and were suffering from PIA," Ted said sounding serious.

"PIA?" Jim asked. He was starting to wonder if he was the subject of some master practical joke.

"Promotion-Induced Amnesia."

"Promotion-Induced Amnesia?" Jim smiled, now convinced that he was the butt of a joke. "Okay man, who put you up to this? It was Derek, wasn't it? Jose?"

"Hey listen, if you think this is a practical joke then the joke is on me. I am stuck with you for as long as it takes to prevent you from getting PIA."

Jim sped into the right lane and made a sharp turn into the empty parking lot of a small restaurant off the highway. He brought the car to a screeching halt, shut the car off, took the keys out of the ignition and bolted from the car.

Ted rolled his eyes. "Why me?" he said, looking up and shaking his head. "Why do I always get the goofy ones? You always give me the assignments that no one else wants."

There was no audible response, but a moment later Ted sighed and said, "Fine, fine, I'll do it." He stepped out of the car and shouted to Jim.

"Get back in the car, dufus."

Jim was pacing like a caged animal. Then he started pointing at Ted and shouting for him to leave his car.

Ted rolled his eyes incredulously and hollered, "No one else can see me but you, so right now everyone passing by thinks you are yelling at your car."

"Hey mister, are you okay?" a young man asked as he drove by slowly.

"I'm trying to get that man to leave me alone!" Jim said before he realized how silly and desperate he sounded.

"What man, mister?"

"I'm talking about that man in my car!" Jim said pointing to his car.

The young man looked at the car and saw only the car. "Sir, there is no one in your car." He rolled up his window and drove away, shaking his head.

"I told you,'" Ted said, shrugging his shoulders. "I'm an *angel*, brainiac. I choose who I will allow to see me. Today, you're the lucky one. So hurry up and get in the car. The sooner we get this done, the sooner I can be out of your hair."

Ted leaned back in his seat and puffed on his cigar.

Jim approached the car and looked inside the window. He studied Ted for the first time. He appeared to be in his fifties. He was balding, and the hair he had left was salt and pepper colored with a beard to match. He wore deck shoes with no socks, a pair of khaki pants, and a golf polo shirt. He had a bit of a beer gut but was in fair shape for a man – or angel – of his age. Jim furled his brow and stared hard at the man. Ted reminded him of a cross between Alan King, Don Rickles and George Burns.

"Anyone ever tell you that you look like Alan King?" Jim asked.

"I get that a lot."

"So, you're an angel?"

"Not quite! Working on it though," Ted said, looking straight ahead.

"So, you are a cigar-smoking angel?"

"It's hell! I've been puffing on the same cigar for twenty years and I get nothing: no smoke, no flavor, just air."

"Why don't you quit?" Jim asked sarcastically.

"I don't quit, kid. Quitting is for losers!"

"Okay, so what are you supposed to do for me?" Jim asked.

"Simple. Help you avoid getting a leader's lobotomy and keep you from falling prey to PIA as so many other leaders do, day in and day out."

"What's in it for you?" The businessman in Jim was coming out.

"I get my wings," Ted said sarcastically.

"Oh, my goodness! Really?" Jim asked with childlike wonder.

"No, not really," Ted grunted. "What do you think this is, 'It's A Wonderful Life?' You are not Jimmy Stewart, I am not Clarence, and we are definitely not in Bedford Falls. Just get in the car."

Jim stepped back from the car. "This is not happening," he said, shutting his eyes tightly. "This is not happening."

"Okay, I don't have time for this. I'm leaving," Ted said. The car's engine magically roared on and the car began moving forward.

Jim looked down at the car keys still in his hand, and sprinted after the car. "No wait, wait! Ted! I believe you."

"Okay then, let's go. You're going to be late for dinner."

Jim settled uneasily into the driver's seat, took a deep breath and pulled back onto the highway. He looked straight ahead and did not even blink.

"Look," Ted said, finally breaking the silence. "I know this is a bit strange for you."

"Strange?" Jim shot back nervously. "Why would this be strange? I mean just because a ghost…"

"Angel," Ted said.

"Sorry," Jim continued. "I mean, yeah, it's really common for an angel to simply appear in my car. It happens every day."

"No need to get snippy, Jimmy," Ted smiled. "Is it okay if I call you Jimmy?"

Jim looked at him with contempt.

"Okay, note to self; don't call him Jimmy," Ted said, as an elegant little leather bound notebook and quill pen magically appeared, floating in thin air in front of Ted's face. The pen glided across the page under its own power and scribed the words Ted had just spoken; then both the pen and the notebook disappeared.

"I'll leave you now for a while," Ted said. "I just wanted to drop in, introduce myself and get you over the initial shock."

"Don't rush back," Jim said under his breath, relieved that his hallucination was coming to an end.

"What's that, Jimmy?"

"I said, 'how about that.'" He looked to his right and found the passenger seat empty. Ted had vanished.

————————

By the time Jim and Marisol returned home after the show, Jim had forgotten all about Ted. He smiled to himself as he lay down next to his wife. She was already half asleep.

"Thanks for a great night, dear," he said softly into her ear.

"You're welcome, Mr. Vice President," she said in a whisper as she slipped into a cozy sleep.

Jim went to bed confident that all was well, and that tomorrow was going to be a great day.

————————

"Wake up, sleeping beauty," Ted said in a raspy voice.

Jim woke up, startled. "You? I thought you were…"

"Gone?" Ted said. "No, but you will wish I was gone soon. Now get up, we've got work to do."

Jim looked at the alarm clock. "It's 4:30 in the morning, and please keep your voice down or you'll wake my wife."

"She can't hear me, genius. Remember – angel, kinda-like-a-ghost? Now get down to your office. It's time for lesson number one on what you should not forget as a leader."

For the first time, Jim was intrigued by what Ted had to say. If this was a figment of his imagination, he might as well go with it.

By the time Jim got downstairs to his home office, Ted was already sitting on the desk.

He pointed at the desk chair. "Sit," he ordered. Jim complied.

"Now pay attention, buttercup. Much of what I am going to tell you will seem simple and even trivial. But mark my words; these simple truths are often overlooked by the most seasoned leaders, and even by some good ones."

Jim leaned forward in the chair and stared intently at Ted. "Now, the notebook in front of you," Ted continued.

Jim looked down. There was nothing in front of him. "I don't see a notebook."

"That's because it's invisible," Ted explained. "You will only see it when I give you something to write in it, or when you need to be reminded of something I told you to write down. Got it?"

"Got it," Jim repeated, only half confident that he indeed had it.

"Okay, leaders who suffer from PIA exhibit many symptoms, most of which are visible to everyone around them except for themselves. My job is to teach you about the rules you must never forget as a leader. If you keep these rules in mind at all times, you will avoid the leader's lobotomy and you will not die from PIA. Think of these lessons as antidotes to a terrible poison. Follow me so far?"

"I think so."

"Good. Now take your invisible pen."

There was now a fancy leather-bound notebook and a beautiful gold and white feathered pen on the desk in front of him. Jim reached for the pen and as he picked it up, he noticed a glow coming from it. He smiled.

"It's pretty cool, right?" Ted said.

"Yeah. Cool."

"Okay Jimbo, what's the very first thing you must never forget as a leader?"

Jim squinted as he searched his mind for an answer. He had read all the best books on the subject. This was his chance to really impress Ted.

"Always do the right thing," Jim announced proudly. Ted stared at him, expressionless. Jim realized that this was not the answer Ted was looking for.

"Set organizational priorities?" Ted just stared at Jim.

"Direct, align, and motivate people?" Jim said, now grasping for an answer that would get Ted to stop staring at him.

"I told you that these rules were going to be simple, trivial, and in some cases painfully obvious. Try again. What was the first thing you wanted to know from any new leader you ever worked for?"

"I wanted to know where he wanted to take the organization!" Jim answered. "What his vision was for the organization."

"Bingo! He can be taught after all!" Ted mocked Jim playfully, dancing around to the other side of the desk. Both Ted and Jim laughed.

"Write this down: *A leader must never forget that having a clear vision is of paramount importance!*"

Jim wrote on the magic notebook with the magic pen, and gold ink captured the thought on the very first page of the notebook.

"How many times did you and your buddies at work sit in the cafeteria and complain that your boss had no clear vision? Even you guys were confused about where you all were driving the organization. Remember?"

Jim nodded in affirmation. It was true. Many times he and his colleagues spoke of that very issue.

"Don't ever forget that, as a leader, having a clear vision is an absolute must. Got that?"

"I got it!" Jim said confidently.

Jim stared at Ted waiting for him to continue.

"What are you waiting for then, sleeping beauty? Get to work. What's your vision? Think about it. Write it down. I'm going back to bed."

With that, Ted disappeared, and Jim was left alone with only the glow of his magic pen to illuminate the darkness around him.

"What's my vision?" Jim asked himself. He settled back in his chair to think about it.

CHAPTER 1

The Reunion

Eight Years Later

Marisol and Jim Givens could hardly believe it as they watched their daughter Michelle blow out the candles on her 8th birthday cake. They looked at each other with a smile and knew that they were both thinking the same thing: where was all the time going?

As Michelle huffed over the candles, three camera flashes went off simultaneously, blinding Marisol, Jim and Michelle. The little girl squealed with glee as her parents kissed her, one on each cheek. The cameras flashed again, freezing the moment in time.

"Jim, can you keep the kids busy while I get the cake and ice cream dished out?" Marisol asked politely, although it was not meant as a question.

"Sure," Jim said. He was happy to play the role of party clown and entertainer for his little girl and her ten giggling friends. "Let's go, guys. Last one to the slide is a rotten egg!" Ten motivated children bolted from the deck and ran, with Jim chasing them all the way.

Grandma and Grandpa, along with other family and friends, watched and took dozens of pictures and video as Jim played with the children.

15

The backyard had been transformed into an amusement park. They had a huge inflatable bouncy gym, a slide, and a caterpillar run. There was a giant twister game, and of course, old-fashioned favorites like pin-the-tail-on-the-donkey and the ever popular piñata.

Jim ran the kids until they were all exhausted. He enjoyed it as much as they did. And what was his reward? Michelle ran as fast as she could and jumped into his arms and said: "This is the best birthday party ever, Daddy! Thank you. You're the best daddy in the world!"

"Come get some cake and ice cream!" Marisol shouted from the kitchen window. All ten children screamed with excitement and stampeded toward the door. Jim was right behind them, grinning from ear to ear.

———————

Several hours later, the house was quiet. Michelle was sleeping soundly, exhausted after a full day of playing and laughing. Jim's in-laws had retired to their guest room, and Marisol was soaking in a hot bubble bath.

Jim was in his office downloading the pictures and video from three digital cameras. The day's activities had been captured from every angle.

"She sure is a beautiful little girl," The raspy deep voice came from the dark side of Jim's office.

Jim nearly fell off his chair. The initial scare only lasted a second as he almost immediately recognized the voice.

"Ted? Is that you?" Jim's voice betrayed his excitement.

"Who else would it be?" Ted responded, as the table lamp next to his chair in the corner magically came on.

"You old dog!" Jim yelled with pure happiness. He realized he might be heard upstairs so he immediately lowered his voice. "You old dog! What the heck are you doing here? What has it been, seven or eight years since I've seen you?"

"Almost eight," Ted replied. "But I've been watching you all along, Jimmy boy."

"Look at you. You look exactly the same! Don't CGA's get older?"

"First of all, you know I don't like the term Corporate Guardian Angels, aka CGA's. It's silly. And no, we don't get older. You, on the other hand, are looking older. A touch of gray on the sides," Ted said motioning to Jim head.

"Marisol says it make me look distinguished," replied Jim, running his hands across the both sides of his head.

"That's a wife's kind way of saying you're getting old," Ted shot back.

"Hey, I'm only forty-seven," Jim said defensively.

Both men looked at each other.

"It's good to see you, Ted."

"You too, kid," Ted said warmly. "You remember how we first met?"

"How could I forget? You nearly scared me to death when you appeared out of nowhere in my car. It was the day I was officially promoted to VP of Operations. Hard to believe more than eight years have passed already!"

"I wish you could have seen your face. That was really funny."

"So who sent you this time?" Jim asked. "Was it Maryann again?"

"Maryann is enjoying her early retirement. She is traveling through Europe and does not have a care in the world. Sends her best to you and the family," Ted said with a grin.

"So it *was* her!" Jim exclaimed.

"She is still a stockholder in the company, and now that you are going to be the president, she wants to make sure to protect her investment even more."

"You really do know everything, don't you?" Jim said. His appointment as the new president of ITA had not yet been made public.

Ted smiled.

"So, do I need a remedial program to avoid the leader's lobotomy again? Are you worried about me suffering from Promotion-Induced Amnesia?"

Jim asked, confident that he had not forgotten the important lessons he learned from Ted some eight years back.

"Actually, my boy, you've been doing quite well in those areas. I've been proud of you." Ted paused. "Most of the time anyway."

Jim could tell that Ted had something up his sleeve.

"I tried my best," Jim said in his defense.

"And you've done well, like I said."

"But?"

"No buts. Now it's time to take a hard look in the mirror, Jimmy boy."

A small golden mirror materialized before Jim's eyes. He instinctively reached for the glowing object.

"A magic mirror?" Jim asked with boyish anticipation. "As in 'mirror mirror on the wall'?"

"This is not a fairy tale, and you are certainly no Snow White," Ted said with his usual sarcasm. "The mirror does have some magic powers, however. It will answer the right questions with brutal honesty."

"Cool," Jim said as he smiled.

"You heard what I said?" Ted asked sternly.

"What?" Jim asked, worried he had missed something important.

"You have to ask the right questions," Ted said again, this time with greater emphasis.

Jim waited for the obvious next statement from Ted. "Well?" he asked finally.

"Well, what?" Ted replied.

"How do I know what questions to ask?"

Ted smiled broadly.

Jim nodded his head knowingly and said, "School's in session, right?"

"Ding, ding!" Ted said as he rang the imaginary school bell. "Good leaders who want to become great leaders have to do two things. First, they have to practice all the principles of a Legacy Leader. Next, they have to take a critical look at their skills, and implement a personal continuous improvement plan."

"That's a tall order, my friend," Jim said.

Ted pointed both hands at Jim and said, "That's why you get paid the big bucks, kiddo. Let's start with a quick review. What are the fundamental skills of a Legacy Leader?"

Jim squinted at Ted, and then he smiled. "I know," he said, "why don't we ask the mirror?"

"Marvelous idea," Ted said.

"Mirror mirror in my hand," Jim began, trying not to laugh. Ted rolled his eyes and sighed. "Mirror mirror in my hand, what are the fundamental skills of a Legacy Leader?"

The magic mirror began to glow, and Jim could see words coming into focus.

"What do you see?" Ted asked, despite already knowing the answer.

Jim read the words out loud:

> *The Legacy Leader is: a person of character, vision, credibility and trustworthiness. A builder of achieving organizations. A motivator and good communicator. The Legacy Leader is a mentor and sponsor whose focus is on people development. The Legacy Leader is an agent of breakthrough thinking and change.*

The Legacy Leader is: a person of character, vision, credibility and trustworthiness. A builder of achieving organizations. A motivator and good communicator. The Legacy Leader is a mentor and sponsor whose focus is on people development. The Legacy Leader is an agent of breakthrough thinking and change.

"It's pretty cool, right?" Ted asked with a broad smile.

Jim was smitten with the mirror. He asked another question: "How do I avoid Promotion-Induced Amnesia and the Leader's Lobotomy?"

The words on the mirror disappeared as others began to come into focus. Jim started reading as soon as he could make out the new words.

The Legacy Leader avoids PIA by having a vision, communicating and listening well, dealing with corporate jealousy and diversity in the organization, focusing on people development, ensuring that strategy and team culture are aligned, and building a L.E.G.A.C.Y.

Jim laughed out loud. "Hey, that's *my* acronym! I came up with L.E.G.A.C.Y. It was the last thing you and I talked about eight years ago."

"I stole your idea," Ted said proudly.

"What does the acronym L.E.G.A.C.Y. stand for?" Jim asked, ignoring Ted's confession. Once again, words began to appear on the mirror and Jim read them out loud:

Leaders must consider what they want their legacy to be, and act in ways consistent with that on a daily basis. L is for Lead and Love. E is for Educate, Evolve and Empower. G is for Give and Grow. A is for Attitude. C is for Create. Y is for You.

Jim laughed again. He was really enjoying his new toy.

"Ask the right question, and you will get a very good answer," Ted said.

"Got it," Jim said. "Where do we go from here?"

"You are a good leader, Jim. You've learned how to put into practice many of the leadership fundaments of a Legacy Leader. You can be proud of the results you have helped your organization achieve over the years. Importantly, you've avoided the pitfalls of the Leader's Lobotomy. Now it's time to sharpen the blade. There's only one way to do that."

Jim suspected what would be next. "Take a hard look in the mirror?"

"That's right. You are your own toughest critic. If you are honest with yourself and think hard about the areas we are going to cover, I guarantee you will be better off when it's all said and done."

Jim needed no convincing. He trusted Ted. "I'm in. Let's get started."

"We start at the beginning, then," Ted explained. "The first thing you must evaluate yourself against are the Six C's of Leadership."

Jim looked perplexed. "What are the six C's?"

Ted smiled and winked at Jim, and as he did he began to slowly fade away… until he vanished.

"Hey!" Jim complained. "Hey Ted, come back here! What are the Six…?" Jim stopped mid-sentence and smiled at himself. He looked at the mirror that was still in his right hand.

"What are the Six C's of Leadership?" he said to the mirror. Words slowly came into focus.

Although he was nowhere to be seen, Ted's voice thundered, "Start with the first one, kid!"

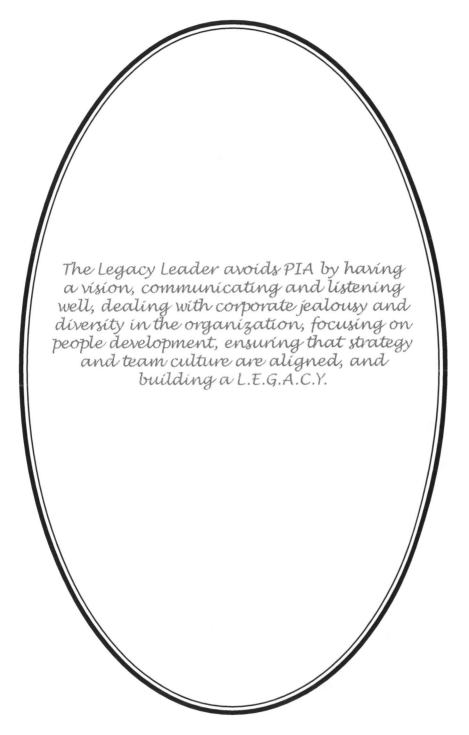

The Legacy Leader avoids PIA by having a vision, communicating and listening well, dealing with corporate jealousy and diversity in the organization, focusing on people development, ensuring that strategy and team culture are aligned, and building a L.E.G.A.C.Y.

Leaders must consider what they want their legacy to be, and act in ways consistent with that on a daily basis.

- *L is for Lead and Love*
- *E is for Educate and Empower*
- *G is for Give and Grow*
- *A is for Attitude*
- *C is for Create*
- *Y is for You*

CHAPTER 2

The SixC's of Leadership

The drive into the office seemed shorter than usual for Jim. He realized that he had been lost in thought the entire trip. Luckily it was still early and there was hardly anyone else on the road. As he parked his car, he recalled how he felt the first day he came to the office after his promotion to VP eight years earlier. Back then they still had reserved parking spots for the executives. He thought of how dumb it was to have them at all.

"We've come along way in just a few years," Jim said out loud, although he was alone.

"So have you!" Ted said from the back seat.

Jim jumped slightly, startled by the familiar voice coming from the back of his car. He looked in the rearview mirror and saw Ted smiling broadly at him.

"I guess I have to get used to you just popping in whenever you feel like it?"

"For now, yes you do," Ted said. "Now I have a question for you. What was on your mind just now when you said, 'we've come a long way'?"

"Lots of things. The company has grown steadily over the years. We are number one or two in most markets we compete in. We have a great team of professionals. Our turnover rates are low, manufacturing efficiencies are high, and our costs are being well managed."

"You sound like a company president already. Go on," Ted urged.

"Our organizational culture is one of open communications. And office politics? Well, they are there of course, but they are not nearly as bad as they once were."

"Sounds pretty good to me," Ted said sincerely.

"Importantly, I think we are doing a good job with people development and giving our folks stretch assignments," Jim said with pride.

"So you now have a great opportunity to build on your predecessor's legacy, right?"

"That will not be easy. He did an outstanding job and is leaving the company in great shape," Jim said as he felt the weight of that statement settle onto his shoulders.

"No better time than now for you to take a good inventory of your strengths and skills as a leader and do a brutally honest self-assessment," Ted said. "Get to it, Jim. You have some work to do."

A short while later, with a cup of coffee in hand, Jim sat quietly in his new office. He allowed himself a moment to enjoy his surroundings. He smiled. There had been times when he did not think he would ever get a chance to sit in that chair as president of the company. There had been other times when he was convinced he did not even want to be president!

He had been giving thought to the Six C's of Leadership, and in a whisper he asked himself, "What are the Six C's of Leadership?" Just as he said those words, the magic mirror appeared on his desk, and the answer came into focus.

Jim looked intently at the mirror and contemplated the words. He thought hard about how he could measure himself against them.

"Don't over analyze it, kid," came Ted's voice from nowhere in particular. "Remember, leadership is not rocket science!"

Jim grabbed a notepad and began to write down a series of questions.

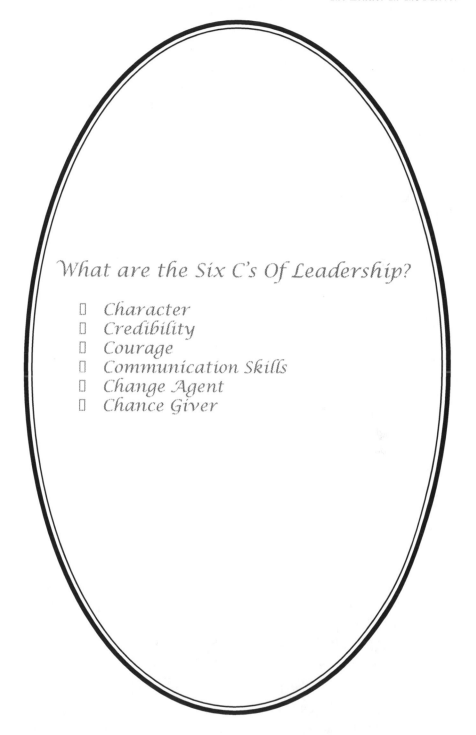

What are the Six C's Of Leadership?

- ☐ *Character*
- ☐ *Credibility*
- ☐ *Courage*
- ☐ *Communication Skills*
- ☐ *Change Agent*
- ☐ *Chance Giver*

CHAPTER 3

Character and Credibility

Jim thought about the kinds of questions that would be important to answer in order to measure a person's character. He paused for a moment and was tempted do a Google search on the word *character* to see what would come up.

"No Googling," Ted's voice thundered. "You already know the answer."

"Okay, okay," Jim replied. He wrote:

Men and women of character:

- *Hold themselves and others to the highest ethical behavior standards*
- *Speak the truth transparently*
- *Gain and keep the trust of others*
- *Treat all with respect and dignity*
- *Hold themselves accountable to results*
- *Stay true to their core principles and values*

As he finished writing, he put the pen down and read the statements carefully.

"Good, Jimmy boy," Ted said as he materialized in the chair next to Jim's desk. "Don't overcomplicate this process, son. Leave that to the psychologists and consultants who make a living developing complicated tools to try to pigeonhole people into personality types."

"Are you saying things like Myers-Briggs, Insights and 360-Degree Assessments are bogus?" Jim asked incredulously.

"Not necessarily. I think they do offer good insight, but what I am saying is that sometimes people tend to overcomplicate things. If you ask and answer the right questions about who you are as a person and a leader, you have a better chance of ultimately behaving in ways that will make you more effective."

Jim looked at Ted with some skepticism.

"Think about it," Ted continued. "Look at the six statements you've just written down. Boiled down, they say that a person of character is accountable for their behavior and the results, speaks the truth, is trustworthy, treats people respectfully, and is true to their personal compass."

Jim smiled. "When you put it that way, it sounds good. But how do I know if I measure up? Do I ask some people to rate me on these?"

"It never hurts to get feedback from others. If you ask the right questions of the right people, you will get some useful insight. But who knows you better than you? If you answer those questions yourself and are brutally honest, you will get much more out of the exercise."

Jim reflected on Ted's words for a moment.

"Who would know better than you if you have behaved ethically in all occasions?" Ted continued. "Ask yourself this: *have I done anything that I would not want made public the next day? Would I want to have to explain this to my wife or my friends?*"

"I see where you're going with this," Jim said, interrupting Ted. "Have I spoken the truth in all occasions? Have I always treated people respectfully? Have I ever compromised on my values?"

"Right! Only you can answer those questions. Now, this is not an exercise for you to then kick yourself in the butt and go all Catholic on me with *mia culpa, mia culpa*," Ted said pounding his chest. "These may be great questions to ask yourself in a retrospective way, but they are much more effective as strong daily reminders of how you must behave going forward – as guiding lights, so to speak."

"That makes sense to me. If I make certain that my behaviors and those of others are always ethical, if I treat people with dignity, speak the truth as transparently as possible, and always hold myself accountable, then people will see me as a man of character."

Ted smiled and nodded. "Now you are getting it. That's why you look in the mirror, because the best assessment is the one we give ourselves – but only if we are able to be honest and don't hold on to some romantic notion of who we think we are, or how we think we are perceived. Instead, you have to take a realistic view of your skills, motives, and behaviors without allowing an inflated ego to get in the way."

"So it's safe to assume that this exercise wouldn't work for Donald Trump, then?" Jim asked with a smile.

Ted rolled his eyes. "Absolutely not! It's impossible for this self-assessment to work for a person who thinks they can do no wrong, or for one who is so in love with his persona that he only looks in the mirror to check his hair."

"I understand. Brutal honesty with self is the key to a good personal assessment."

"You got it, Jimmy boy. Good. Moving on to the second C," Ted said.

"Credibility," Jim said. "I love what Steven M. R. Covey has to say about credibility in his book *The Speed of Trust.*"

"I do too, so why re-invent the wheel?"

"Magic Mirror, what are the Four Cores of Credibility according to Covey?"

The magic mirror began to glow as the words came into focus.

"I love this thing!" Jim said, sounding more like a ten-year old boy than the forty seven-year old president of a major corporation.

The words in the mirror said:

What are the Four Cores of Credibility according to Covey?

- *Are you a person of integrity?*
- *What is your agenda?*
- *Are you staying current and up-to-date?*
- *What is your track record?*

Jim studied the words on the mirror.

"Those are simple truths, right? Ted asked. "Just four basic questions. First, are you a person with integrity? In other words, are your behaviors congruent?"

"Do I say what I do, and do what I say?" Jim added.

"Precisely. Are you walking the talk? Second, what's your agenda?"

"Am I open about what I am trying to do?"

"Right again. Who can answer that question?"

"Only I can, because no one – except maybe you, of course – knows what I am really thinking."

"Bingo! But your actions will eventually betray your true intent and agenda if they are not consistent with your words. That's the way it always works. Leaders fall into that trap all the time. Third, are you staying current and up-to-date?"

"Meaning, am I up to speed with technology and industry trends, global business dynamics, and that sort of thing?"

"What are the Four Cores of Credibility according to Covey?"

- ☐ *Are you a person of integrity?*
- ☐ *What is your agenda?*
- ☐ *Are you staying current and up-to-date?*
- ☐ *What is your track record?*

"Yes! Also, are you evolving and growing? Your followers will take note of that as well. Finally, number four, what is your track record? In the end, people want to follow leaders who make things happen – leaders who can point to a successful winning record."

"That's good stuff, Ted," Jim said enthusiastically.

"You sound surprised," Ted said with a hint of sarcasm. He continued, "First, think about those four questions, contemplate them for a while and answer them honestly. After that you can move on to the question of trust."

"Good to see you've not lost your touch for coaching and mentoring. I'm surprised you've not been promoted to Senior Executive Corporate Guardian Angel."

"Again with the CGA stuff? I'm outta here," Ted said as he vanished.

"Hey, don't go away mad," said Jim with a broad smile.

"Just finish the work on credibility, smarty pants," Ted voice thundered louder than usual. "Then tackle the trust question."

Jim forwarded his phone to Peggy, his administrative assistant, and decided to spend the next hour reflecting on the four questions.

The day flew by, like most days. It was almost 6:45 p.m. before Jim finally walked out of his office and made his way across the parking lot to his car. As he approached, Ted materialized, sitting on the hood of his recently acquired late model BMW. "Hey," Jim hollered playfully from a distance before remembering that he was the only one who could see Ted sitting there. He lowered his voice and said, "Off the car there, buddy."

"Give me a break. It's only a car."

"Yeah, well, I just waxed it this weekend," Jim complained as he slid into the driver's seat.

In an instant, Ted was next to him. "So how was your day, dear?" he said, in a falsetto voice.

"Oh, boy. I can tell it's going to be an interesting ride home."

"Yes it is. The topic for today, boys and girls, is *trust*. So let's do it, Jimmy.

Tell me all about how you are going to measure yourself against that five letter word."

Jim pulled into traffic and started his answer at the same time.

"Trust is a key element of gaining and keeping credibility. How do I know I have trust from my followers?" Jim asked aloud. "Well, let's ask the magic mirror. What are the behaviors that help gain and maintain trust?"

As Jim spoke those words, the mirror hovered twelve inches away from Ted's face. "Can you read them to me?"

Ted began to read them out loud and Jim immediately recognized them as the thirteen behaviors that Covey outlined in his book as those that consistently lead to trust.

The words on the mirror read:

To gain and keep trust, do I…?
- *Engage in Straight Talk*
- *Demonstrate Respect*
- *Create Transparency*
- *Right Wrongs*
- *Show Loyalty*
- *Deliver Results*
- *Get Better*
- *Confront Reality*
- *Clarify Expectations*
- *Practice Accountability*
- *Listen First*
- *Keep Commitments*
- *Extend Trust*

As Ted read the last of the statements, he asked, "So, what now?"

Jim thought about it for a moment and decided that the best way to evaluate himself against these was to simply put the words "Do I" in front of each statement and answer the question for himself.

"Well done, Mr. President," Ted said.

"I did not say anything yet."

"I read your mind," Ted said with a smirk.

"Now you can read my mind, too?"

"New trick we learned at the CGA Academy. You have some work to do on this trust issue over the next couple of days. Don't just ask yourself the questions. Take it a step further and come up with examples of where you think you've done it well and where you could have done it better. Then commit yourself to improving one or two of them at a time."

"Got it," Jim said as he gave Ted a smart military salute.

"Bye-bye, sweetheart," Ted said, blowing Jim a kiss as he faded away.

Jim knew that this assignment would take some time. He really needed to think about each of these statements carefully. He also decided that he would check with a few people to be certain that he was not being myopic, too generous or overly critical with his self-assessment.

"To gain and keep trust, do I...?"
- ☐ *Engage in Straight Talk*
- ☐ *Demonstrate Respect*
- ☐ *Create Transparency*
- ☐ *Right Wrongs*
- ☐ *Show Loyalty*
- ☐ *Deliver Results*
- ☐ *Get Better*
- ☐ *Confront Reality*
- ☐ *Clarify Expectations*
- ☐ *Practice Accountability*
- ☐ *Listen First*
- ☐ *Keep Commitments*
- ☐ *Extend Trust*

CHAPTER 4

Courage

A few weeks later

It was a warm and beautiful Sunday morning.

Jim squinted as he came into the sun-filled church lobby as he and Marisol left the 11 a.m. service.

"Jim, can you go pick up Michelle from her classroom?" Marisol asked. "I need to talk to Kay about the church picnic next Sunday."

"Sure, honey," Jim responded. "We'll meet you in the car."

As Jim made his way toward Michelle's Sunday School classroom, he stopped numerous times to say hello to a few folks.

"Hey, Jim," Peter waved over the heads of fellow churchgoers, trying to get Jim's attention as he walked toward him from down the hallway.

"Hi Pete," Jim said with a broad smile.

"I'm holding a spot for you on our next trip to Haiti," said Peter, who was the church's missions pastor. "I'm not letting you off the hook this time, my friend."

"I am in. No excuses this time. I am making this missions trip for sure!"

"That's the spirit! It takes a lot of courage to leave behind the comforts of home for ten days. I promise that you will come back a changed man."

"I am looking forward to it. I'll see you tonight at the planning meeting." Just then, Michelle came running into his arms.

"Daddy!" she squealed.

"Hey, munchkin," Jim said raising her high over his head. "How was Sunday School today?"

"It was great."

"What did you learn about today?"

"Courage," Michelle answered.

Jim smiled. "Courage, huh?"

"Yep. Courage. You want me to tell you what I learned about it?"

"I want you to tell me all about it for sure. Let's get your mommy and you can tell us both in the car, okay?"

As they made their way to the car, Jim could not help but think about the assignment he had received from Ted just the night before.

"I don't believe in coincidences, kid." Jim heard Ted's voice, but did not see him anywhere.

"Daddy, I hear Mr. Ted, but I can't see him," Michelle said as Jim buckled her into the back seat of the car.

"Here I am, sweetheart," Ted said, materializing in the seat next to her. "Is it okay if I ride home with you today?"

"You like Mr. Ted, sweetie?" Jim asked. "Now remember, Mr. Ted is our secret right?"

Michelle nodded an enthusiastic yes. "Will Mommy be able to see you today?"

"Not today honey; just you and your daddy. It's our secret, okay?"

Just then Marisol opened the passenger front door and slid into the car. "Hi baby! How was your Sunday School?"

"I learned about courage, and on the way home I'm going to tell you and Daddy all about it."

"I can't wait," Michelle said with a big smile.

"Me neither," Jim added.

"Me three," Ted said, also with a broad smile on his face.

Michelle squealed with joy again.

"Okay honey, Mommy and Daddy are listening. Tell us what you learned about courage today."

"It's very simple, Daddy," Michelle began, sounding much more mature than her eight years would normally allow. "Courage is just four easy things. First, courage is about doing what is right, even when it's hard to do."

Ted beamed at Michelle like a proud grandfather.

"Number two," Michelle continued. "To have courage means to stand firm." Michelle paused for a moment and then asked, "Daddy, what does 'stand firm' mean? Ms. Shelly explained it but I did not understand."

"Well honey, standing firm means that you stay true to your beliefs. When you know something is right, you defend it, no matter what. If you know something is wrong, you refuse to go along with it, no matter what."

As he explained the concept of standing firm to his daughter, Jim clearly understood the implication of the two first rules of courage to leadership.

Satisfied with her daddy's explanation, Michelle continued telling what she had learned about courage. "Third, to have courage means to say what needs to be said, even if it's not popular."

"That's a great lesson, Michelle," Marisol said proudly.

"Ms. Shelly said that doesn't mean that we have to say things in a mean way. But we have to tell the truth in the nicest way we can, even if it might upset some of our friends."

"Are you paying attention, buttercup?" Ted asked Jim.

That caused Michelle to squeal with laughter again. "You called my daddy buttercup!" she said to Ted.

"Who called your daddy buttercup, honey?" Marisol asked.

Michelle giggled.

"Uh, tell us more about courage, sweetheart," Jim said quickly.

"The last thing we learned is that it takes courage to admit when we make mistakes and to learn from them."

When Michelle finished speaking, Jim and Marisol glanced at each other and smiled.

"From the mouths of babes," Marisol remarked.

"Yeah," Jim said with a sigh.

"School's out, Jimmy boy," Ted said. "You just learned everything a leader needs to know about courage from your eight year old."

Ted blew Michelle a kiss and waved goodbye as he slowly faded away. Michelle giggled again.

Later that afternoon, Jim sat in his study at home and reviewed the lessons on courage with the magic mirror. There were four questions he needed to answer:

> *Do I do what is right, even when it's hard to do?*
>
> *Do I stand firm?*
>
> *Do I say what needs to be said, even when it's not popular?*
>
> *Do I admit and learn from my mistakes?*

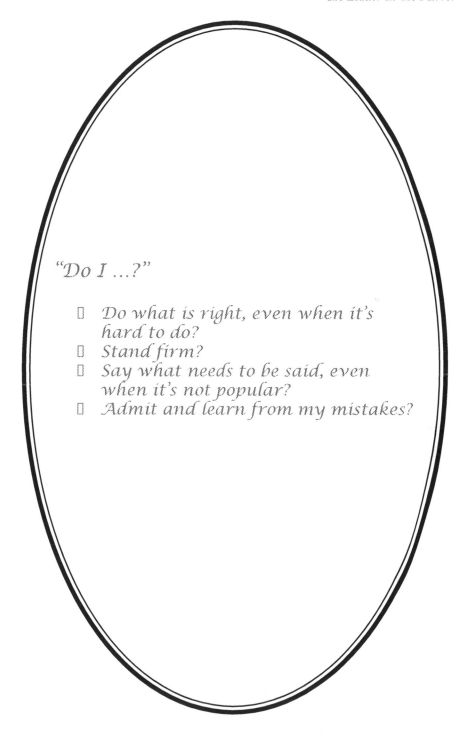

"*Do I ...?*"

- ☐ *Do what is right, even when it's hard to do?*
- ☐ *Stand firm?*
- ☐ *Say what needs to be said, even when it's not popular?*
- ☐ *Admit and learn from my mistakes?*

CHAPTER 5

Communications

The day's calendar was jammed. Jim's first meeting began with a 6 a.m. conference call with the team in Japan. His day would not end until 8 p.m. when he was scheduled to have dinner with an important customer who was visiting the facility for the day.

Jim was lost in thought as he drove to the office that morning. It was pitch black outside and the sun would not be up for a while. He was listening to news on the National Public Radio station when suddenly a program came on that he had never heard before.

"Good morning, listeners," came the announcer's voice. "This is Ken Belcher and today we have a very special guest with us to talk about effective communication for leaders. Please help me welcome Ted."

Jim laughed out loud.

"Good morning, Ken," Ted's unmistakable raspy voice emerged from the speakers and filled Jim's car. "It's a pleasure to be with you today. And good morning to you too, buttercup."

Jim played along and responded to the voice coming from the radio. "Good morning, Ted."

"So tell us, Ted," Ken said seriously, "what are some facts about communications as it relates to leaders?"

"Well, buckle up there Ken, because I am going to come at you fast with this stuff. Extensive data from focus groups and employee surveys clearly shows a common perception that CEO's are not visible or don't care about their organizations. Employees believe that few of their leaders provide sufficient direction, and that they are not always open and honest. They also believe that their leaders sometimes tell lies."

"Well," Ken said. "You certainly get right to the point, don't you?"

Ted continued as if Ken had said nothing. "Leaders are often seen as distorting information – they're viewed as spin doctors, if you will. They often don't seek the opinions of others, nor do they give enough feedback or recognition to their people. Additionally, leaders don't communicate face-to-face with their team as often as they should, choosing instead to rely on impersonal print and electronic formats."

"Wow, slow down there, Ted," Ken complained. "Where are you getting this information?"

"There are numerous sources for this type of information. Any simple internet search will lead you to dozens of papers and reports that substantiate these data," Ted said defensively. "Bottom line is that we can all agree that the leader's ability to effectively communicate is key to a team's success, right?"

"No doubt that is true," Ken agreed.

"Yet so many leaders fall into the traps I just mentioned. Funny thing is that most people only expect and need a few simple things from their leaders when it comes to communicating," Ted said with certainty.

Ken jumped in saying, "You mean, people just want to know where the company is headed and what the overall strategy for the company is? They want to be aware of how the company is doing; of any changes that are happening and how those changes will affect them? Perhaps they want to know what's happening in the competitive environment?"

"See how simple that is?" Ted asked. "It's easy, right? I mean, leaders just have to tell people what's happening, when it's happening, why it's happening, and how it impacts them. Why is that so hard for so many leaders to comprehend?"

As Jim listened intently to the conversation on the radio, he asked himself, "Okay, but even if you do these simple things, how does a person know if they are being effective with their communications?"

"That's the right question, Jimbo," Ted said through the car's speakers.

"Okay," Jim said to the radio. "You want to come out of there now and sit in the car with me?" Ted materialized in the passenger seat.

"So?" Jim asked Ted. "What's the answer?"

"Why are you asking *me*? You have a magic mirror, don't you?"

"Oh yeah, I do!" Jim replied sheepishly. "Mirror, tell me how leaders should measure their effectiveness as communicators?"

"Now wait a moment," Ted interrupted. "Isn't there a question we should ask before that one?"

Jim thought about it for a moment and then said, "Mirror, how should leaders communicate?"

"Now we're going somewhere," Ted said as he reclined his seatback and put his feet up on the dashboard.

The mirror came into view and an image began to form. "Voice mode," Jim commanded, and a smooth female voice began to read the writing on the mirror.

The voice said:

The leader should consider the following factors when communicating:

1. *First, decide what the message you are trying to communicate is.*
2. *Identify specifically your target audience and the best approach to reach them.*
3. *Outline and test your message.*
4. *Design your message (voice, written, or both?)*
5. *Design your communication. Word of mouth can be extremely effective. For example, if you want to address a misconception*

among legislators, the best way might be to enlist a few friends in the legislature to have a conversation with your targets.

6. *Decide how and when to distribute the message.*
7. *Measure the success of the communication.*

"Wow, don't you wish everything was so simple?" Ted asked with his eyes closed.

"Mirror, how do I measure my effectiveness as a leader?" Jim asked next.

The image in the mirror began to change and soon new words came into focus. "Continue in voice mode," Jim said.

The voice read:

To measure their effectiveness as communicators, leaders should answer the following questions:

1. *What are their personal barriers to communications?*
2. *How well do they deal with these communication barriers?*
3. *How well do they listen?*
4. *Do they adjust their style and message to the fit the audience?*
5. *Are they able to remain open-minded?*
6. *Are they consistent with their message?*
7. *Are they candid, honest and always transparent with their communications?*
8. *How well do they apply the KISS principle to communications?*

"I love that last one most of all," Ted said, his eyes still closed. "KISS. Keep It Simple, Stupid!"

Jim nodded in agreement.

"Remember the three rules of communication for a leader?" Ted asked, confident that Jim would recall the answer.

"Communicate to *inform,* not to *impress*; communicate to *clarify,* not to *confuse*; and communicate *directly,* not with *double talk.*"

"Perfect, my boy!"

"Thank you, sir," Jim said proudly.

"Now, what do you want to do with those questions on communications?" Ted asked.

"I have to give them some thought. I have to give special attention to the barriers to communication. I know I have some work to do there."

"Tell me more, Jimmy."

"Well, I know that I have a hard time staying focused on someone's message or presentation if they... have a certain style," Jim said, trying to choose his words carefully.

"You mean when someone is slow or long winded?" Ted said without thinking much about it.

"Especially those types of folks," Jim said with a smile. "I can be a bit impatient with them."

Ted laughed out loud. "A bit? You think? Do I need to show a video clip of you in action, my boy?"

"No no, that is not necessary. Off the top of my head I can think of several cases where I was short with people because of their speaking style."

"That's the secret to a good self-assessment, Jimmy boy. Be honest with yourself. Answer each of these questions carefully and completely. I am sure you can find examples where you did some good stuff. I am just as sure you can come up with an example or two where you did some stupid things."

"No doubt about that," Jim agreed.

"Good. Then you've got your homework assignment, and I have some fishing to do." Ted vanished.

The leader should consider the following factors when communicating:

1. Decide what the message you are trying to communicate is.

2. Identify specifically your target audience and the best approach to reach them.

3. Outline and test your message.

4. Design your message.

5. Design your communication.

6. Decide how and when to distribute the message.

7. Measure the success of the communication.

To measure their effectiveness as communicators, leaders should answer the following questions:

1. *What are their personal barriers to communications?*
2. *How well do they deal with these communication barriers?*
3. *How well do they listen?*
4. *Do they adjust their style and message to the audience?*
5. *Are they able to remain open minded?*
6. *Are they consistent with their message?*
7. *Are they candid, honest and always transparent with their communications?*
8. *How well do they apply the KISS principle to communications?.*

CHAPTER 6

Change Agent

The cafeteria was especially crowded that day.

"It must be raining," Beverly said, smiling at Jim.

"It is raining cats and dogs out there, Bev." Jim had known Beverly for almost fifteen years. For all that time she had worked as the short order cook in the company cafeteria. She had a contagious smile, a cheerful attitude, and she knew everyone in the company by their first name.

"That's why it's so crowded in here today," she said, gently placing a slice of cheese on Jim's burger as it sizzled on the grill top. She didn't even have to ask him if he wanted cheese – she knew exactly how he liked his burger. "Everybody's trying to escape from the rain, so they come see Bev," she said with a loud laugh.

"I'm here rain or shine, Bev!" Gary yelled from the back of the line.

"I love you too, Gary," Bev said, pointing her spatula at him. "But you still have to wait in line for your burger. Don't you worry though; I'll make sure you get extra fries!"

"Hey Bev, what about me?" Nelly asked, grinning.

"What about you? I got a bone to pick with you, young lady. You've not been in here in over a week!" she said as she flipped some burgers on the grill.

"Hey, blame Jim. He has me traveling all over the globe," she said in self-defense.

Beverly turned and gave Jim a motherly look. "Is that true, Mr. Givens?" Her tone was that of a school teacher getting ready to scold a student.

"Well, I guess so. But it's great experience for her," Jim said truthfully.

"Great experience, you say? Just remember this child just got married six months ago. She's got a husband to go home to now. So don't you work her to death, you hear?" Bev put the finishing touches on Jim's burger and handed the plate over to him.

"Yes, ma'am," Jim answered. "Thanks, Bev."

Jim found an empty seat at a table in the back corner of the large room. He recognized many of the faces around the table. It was mostly folks from the production floor.

"Hi folks; do you mind if I join you?" Jim said pleasantly.

"Well, good afternoon, Mr. G," came Bill's thundering voice. Bill was a veteran employee. He was nearing retirement, but had lost none of his enthusiasm for his work or for the people at the company.

"Hi, Bill. How have you been?"

"I'm doing great; just great."

"How's that new baby granddaughter of yours?" Jim asked.

"She's growing like a weed! There is nothing better than being a grandpa. I tell you, I am loving it."

"That's wonderful." Before he sat down, Jim made a quick trip around the table to shake hands with everyone sitting there, and a few folks sitting at tables nearby.

"Hello, I'm Jim," he said when he came to the one person he did not recognize at the table.

"Hello Mr. Givens, my name is Millie Sanchez. It's nice to meet you," the young woman said as she shook Jim's hand.

"Nice to meet you too, Millie. Please call me Jim," he said with a warm smile. "How long have you been with us, Millie?"

"Just started about three months ago," she said nervously.

"That's great. Welcome to the team. Where are you working?"

"I'm a QA tech in Bill's department," she answered.

"Good for you," Jim exclaimed with a broad smile. "I can't think of a better teacher to work for at this company." Jim gave Bill a hearty pat on the back. Bill blushed, but also beamed with pride.

"I agree one hundred percent," Millie said. She was much more relaxed now.

"That's really nice of you to say, Jim," Bill said sincerely.

"I mean it. It's the truth," Jim said emphatically.

Everyone at the table agreed and made supportive comments.

"Enough already!" Bill said modestly. "What's this, a love fest? You won't even miss me when I'm gone in six months."

"You can't retire, Bill," Kevin said. "Mildred will kill you if she has to put up with you all day at home." Everyone laughed.

"Got room for one more?" Lydia asked.

"Absolutely," Bill answered for the group. "We can squeeze. We're all family here."

Lydia put her tray down and sat, greeting everyone in the table.

"Lydia, have you met Millie Sanchez?" Jim asked.

"I did this morning. We had a QA review meeting, and we met there. Good to see you again, Millie," she said, smiling at the young woman.

Lydia was the plant operations manager for the site. She'd been with the company only a few years and was doing a phenomenal job. Jim considered her one of his best hires. Of all of Lydia's great leadership qualities, Jim had been most impressed with her ability to create and manage organizational change.

Before Lydia took over as the new operations manager, the plant was running effectively. But just one year after she arrived, the plant was running at peak efficiency. Jim knew that there was more than a semantics difference between these two words. The difference was evident and had led to significant cost reductions and operational improvements that were clearly making ITA more competitive. Lydia was succeeding where others had attempted and failed. Jim was learning about how to be a leader of change from Lydia – a person he had hired!

Jim took a quick mental inventory of the seven people seated around him. By his estimation, all together there were nearly one hundred years of experience sitting at that table.

Lydia took a quick bite of her sandwich and then said, "Bill, Millie had a phenomenal suggestion this morning during the meeting. I think we need to consider the approach she suggested. I have a feeling it would really drive some significant improvement on how we do our sampling on the T-Line."

The T-Line was ITA's fastest moving production line. It ran only the highest volume products. The T-Line was also usually the constriction point of many of the other production lines, since it manufactured many of the components necessary to make other ITA products.

Due to of its importance, the manufacturing team was usually quite resistant to making too many changes to the T-line.

Millie's eyes lit up when she heard Lydia's comment about her suggestion.

"Kevin," Lydia continued, "what did you think of Millie's idea?"

As the first shift supervisor of the T-Line, Kevin was one of the most knowledgeable people in the company on the line's operations. He had been with ITA for almost twenty years, having started with the company right after high school when he was only eighteen years old.

"Well," Kevin said without hesitating to offer his viewpoint, "I am not a huge fan of making too many changes to the line, as you know, Lydia. You know what I always say…"

"If it ain't broke, don't fix it!" said all the others sitting at the table, in unison.

"Well, that's not a bad way of thinking," Kevin said defensively. "But you know, I think Millie's idea has some merit, and I think we should look at it more carefully."

Lydia saw an opening to affect a positive change, and she pounced on it!

"I'm with you, Kevin. And I agree that 'if it ain't broke don't fix it' is not always a bad way of thinking," she said. Hearing Lydia say that made Kevin feel better. "I also agree that Millie's idea deserves a closer look. Millie, could you take a few minutes now and tell us again how you guys did it in your previous company?"

Millie spent the next five minutes explaining her idea for how to improve the efficiency of product sampling coming off the T-Line.

When she was done, Jim asked, "What do you think that could mean in time savings?"

"I estimate about fifteen minutes per batch," she said confidently.

Bill smiled like a proud father. The rest of the people at the table did a quick mental calculation of what that translated to in overall cost savings.

Bill broke the silence. "We all just did the math right? Fifteen minutes a batch adds up very quickly with the number of batches we have running through there. We are talking about a major cost reduction."

Kevin agreed.

"We all agree that the end-in-mind is to ensure the integrity of the T-Line while improving the sampling efficiencies, right?" Lydia said, wanting to ensure that everyone was aligned to the shared vision of the change that was being proposed.

Kevin agreed emphatically. "Yes," he said, "I agree we want to maintain the integrity first and foremost. We can't afford to have any hiccups in the line. It's too important. So this change needs to be transparent to the production flow."

Everyone nodded in agreement.

"Good," Lydia continued. "We all agree. The line's integrity is paramount. However, let's make sure we challenge the process and be open to experiment and take a few reasonable risks. Agreed?"

Again, everyone nodded in agreement.

"Great. Kevin, I think you and your team are the absolute best to lead this effort. If anyone can judge whether the change we make is the right one, it would be you and your team. Can I count on you for that?"

Kevin beamed with pride. "You got it," he said.

Lydia turned to Millie. "Well, Millie," she said with a broad smile, "it looks like you just talked yourself into a project lead role for this change. Are you up to it?"

"She's more than up to it," Bill answered for Millie.

Millie grinned. "We'll make it happen together," she said.

"This might mean overtime for the guys to try this on some pilot runs over weekends," Kevin said.

Lydia looked at Jim. "Well, Mr. Givens? Are you going to enable this team with a bit of funding?"

"Absolutely!" Jim said without hesitation.

"Okay guys," Lydia announced, "you heard the boss, and he's paying the tab. Millie, can you put together a quick action plan on how we will go about making this change? I'd like to review it with you and Kevin as soon as possible."

"No problem. We'll need to include time for training the production teams on all shifts and the QA techs as well," Millie added.

"Good. Bill, you hired a winner here," Lydia said

"Of course. Would you expect anything else?"

"Not at all!" she said with complete sincerity.

"You guys make this happen within a month, and I will take this team out to dinner," Jim announced.

"Deal!" they all said in unison.

"But we pick the place!" Kevin added. "Last time you took us out to some fancy French place with snails on the menu. I mean it was nice, but snails? I don't think so."

"Fine, you all can choose the place," Jim agreed.

Jim made his way back to his office after lunch. He stopped a few times along the way to drop in and say hello to several folks he had not seen in awhile. He always enjoyed the impromptu short meetings that took place whenever he walked around. Jim knew that helped keep him connected to the organization.

When he finally made it back to his office, he noticed the magic mirror hovering over his desk next to his computer screen.

The words on the mirror were a message from Ted: "That was quite a lesson on creating and managing change!"

Jim knew exactly what Ted was referring to. He had just seen Lydia create a reason for a change, engage the team in the change, outline the vision for the team, define the big picture action plan, ensured management's buy in and support, and enabled the team to take action. Moreover, she had done it all in a matter of thirty minutes over lunch.

Ted materialized in his favorite spot on the couch in Jim's office.

"She was brilliant, wasn't she?" he asked.

"Lydia? Yes, she was. She has a way of energizing a team to adopt an idea, make it their own, and drive changes," Jim said.

"Did you notice her approach, Jimmy boy?"

"Yes I did."

"It was impressive the way she accomplished so many things in such a short period of time. First, she managed to motivate Millie. As a new employee she's got to be feeling very good right now. Second, she managed to involve Kevin!"

"I know!" Jim agreed. "Kevin is usually quite resistant to change, especially on the T-Line."

"Yes, but she made him a part of the process and the decision making. In fact, she made him the co-lead on the project! Brilliant!"

"Sure was. She even roped me in with the overtime cost," he said with a smile.

"Well of course she did. That's how she secured management's support for the change. Otherwise the change can't happen," Ted said emphatically. "Then she enabled the team and encouraged them to make it happen. It was perfect execution of creating change and managing through it."

"So simple, too," Jim added.

"What else did you notice about this particular change?" Ted asked.

"It was small in scope, but large in impact," Jim said.

"Bingo! Give that man a cigar. Think about that Jimmy! It was small in scope, meaning easy to execute with relatively low risk of failure, but the impact of the change will be huge to your organization."

"That's been the key to her success all along, hasn't it? Not necessarily huge, sweeping changes, but smaller ones sustained over time that have added up to a big impact."

As Jim said those words, their significance sank in for both men. "She's a change agent," Jim concluded.

"I love my job!" Ted said. And then he disappeared.

Jim sat for a few moments thinking about what he had just said. "Mirror, how should a leader measure their success as a change agent?"

The mirror immediately began glowing as words came into focus.

> *To measure their effectiveness as change agents, leaders should first consider The Five Practices and Ten Commandments of Leadership as*

outlined by Kouzer and Posner in their classic book "The Leadership Challenge".

Jim studied the words on the screen and kept waiting for a few moments thinking that there would be more to the answer. "Mirror, according to Kouzer and Posner, what are the Five Practices and Ten Commandments of Leadership?" he asked.

Once again the mirror was glowing.

According to Kouzer and Posner, The Five Practices are:

1. *Model the way*
2. *Inspire a shared vision*
3. *Challenge the process*
4. *Enable others to act*
5. *Encourage the heart*

The Ten Commandments of Leadership are:

1. *Find your voice by clarifying your personal values*
2. *Set the example by aligning actions with shared values*
3. *Envision the future by imagining exciting possibilities*
4. *Enlist others in the common vision*
5. *Search for opportunities by seeking innovative ways to change, grow and improve*
6. *Experiment and take risks by constantly generating small wins and learning from mistakes*
7. *Foster collaboration by promoting cooperative goals and building trust*
8. *Strengthen others by sharing power*
9. *Recognize contributions*
10. *Celebrate the values and victories by creating a spirit of community*

Jim studied the words for a long time. These were good. Very good, he thought.

"Mirror," he said at last, "what questions must a leader answer to evaluate their effectiveness as a change agent?"

The mirror answered:

To measure effectiveness as a change agent, the leader must answer the following questions:

How well do I model the way I want people to behave relative to change?

How effectively do I communicate and inspire a shared vision?

Do I challenge existing processes and encourage others to do the same?

How do I support and enable teams to act?

Do I acknowledge and accept risks?

How well do I tolerate failure?

Do I effectively encourage people to change and recognize them for accepting change?

Jim realized he had much work to do.

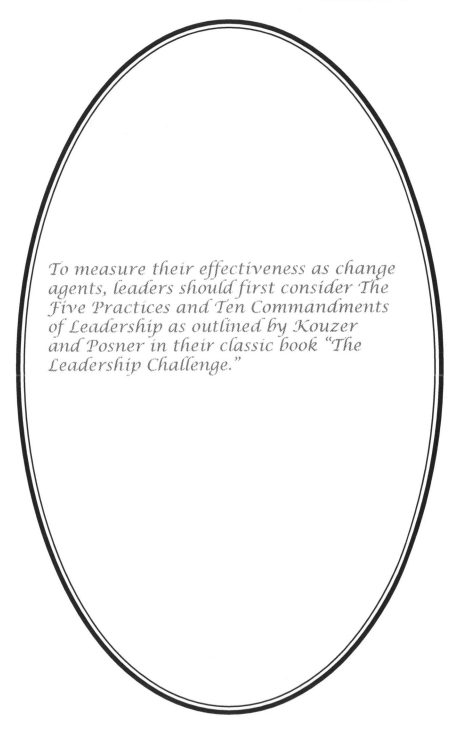

To measure their effectiveness as change agents, leaders should first consider The Five Practices and Ten Commandments of Leadership as outlined by Kouzer and Posner in their classic book "The Leadership Challenge."

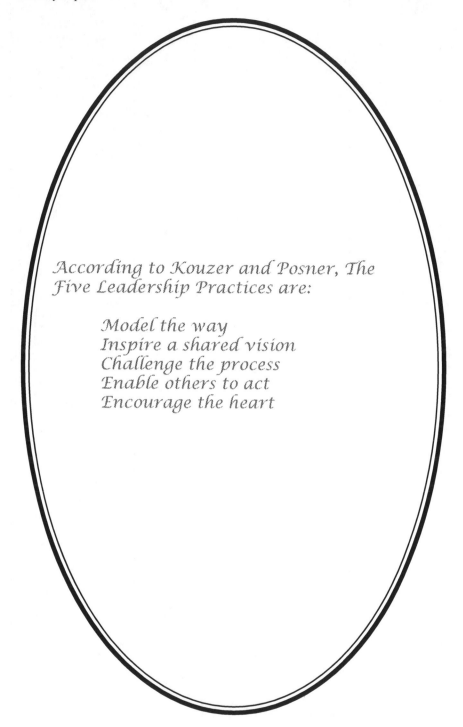

According to Kouzer and Posner, The
Five Leadership Practices are:

Model the way
Inspire a shared vision
Challenge the process
Enable others to act
Encourage the heart

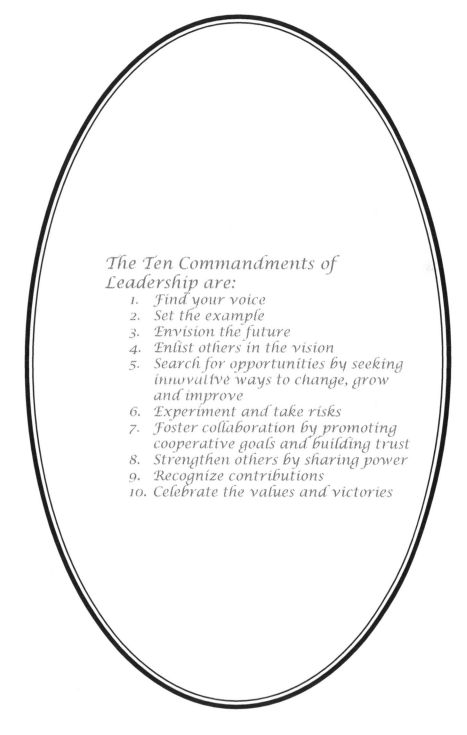

The Ten Commandments of
Leadership are:
1. Find your voice
2. Set the example
3. Envision the future
4. Enlist others in the vision
5. Search for opportunities by seeking
   innovative ways to change, grow
   and improve
6. Experiment and take risks
7. Foster collaboration by promoting
   cooperative goals and building trust
8. Strengthen others by sharing power
9. Recognize contributions
10. Celebrate the values and victories

To measure their effectiveness as a change agent, the leader must answer the following questions:

- *How well do I model the way to behave relative to change?*
- *How effectively do I communicate and inspire a shared vision?*
- *Do I challenge existing processes and encourage others to do the same?*
- *How do I support and enable teams to act?*
- *Do I acknowledge and accept risks?*
- *How well do I tolerate failure?*
- *Do I effectively encourage people to change and recognize them for accepting change?*

CHAPTER 7

Chance Giver

The vibration of the Blackberry phone hanging from his belt told him that he was getting an e-mail. He resisted the temptation to reach for it immediately, but could not help wondering who was sending him a message at 10 p.m. on a Sunday night. After a few minutes, he reached for the phone and read the short message.

"Jim," Marisol complained. "Give it a rest. Enjoy the movie!"

Jim complied and put the phone back in its holster and returned his attention to the large screen in the dark movie theater.

Later that evening, Jim was sitting in the study checking e-mails on his laptop.

"What's so important that it can't wait until tomorrow, Jim?" Marisol asked, although it was more of a request that he spend the time with her than with the computer.

"I'm just going to respond to one message. I promise, just this one. I got an e-mail from Larry and I want to get back to him before morning."

"How's he doing?" Marisol asked with genuine concern. She had met Larry more than ten years prior, when he was a young intern working for Jim.

"He's good. He's being offered a position with a company in Brussels and he wants to talk about it with me before making his final decision."

"Brussels! Wow, that's great. But he's only been in his current job about two years, right?"

Jim nodded. "Actually he has been there less than two years. He's been there about eighteen months. He's in town for some meetings, and he is hoping we can get together to talk about it."

"Why don't you invite him over to dinner tomorrow and you guys can spend some quality time together," Marisol suggested.

"That's a great idea. I'll do that," Jim said as he typed the message.

"Larry is a good kid," Marisol said. "He reminds me a lot of you when you were his age."

Jim smiled. "Yeah, sometimes he's too much like me, making some of the same mistakes I made. He's a bit impatient and hard-charging."

"Hey, those are not bad traits," Marisol pointed out. "They made you the success you are today, right?"

"Yes, but that's because I had some great coaching and mentoring along the way. People like Maryann and Ted who kept me on the narrow path."

"Maryann, of course. I agree with that. But who's Ted?" Marisol asked curiously. "Michelle has mentioned a Mr. Ted also."

"Oh, just a man at work who's been helping me out," Jim said evasively.

"Tell her the truth, Jimbo. She can take it," Ted's voice came from his usual spot near the chair in the corner of the room.

"Just a man? I thought I knew most of the people you work with. We've had a dozen parties here at the house for your team members and I've never met a man named Ted," Marisol said, suspicion creeping into her voice.

"I'll introduce you sometime," Jim said as he finished typing the message to Larry and hitting the send key.

Just then Michelle called out from her bedroom.

"Mommy, I'm thirsty," she hollered.

"Okay baby. Mommy is coming," Marisol turned to Jim.

"You're keeping secrets, Mr. Givens. I expect you to fess up ASAP," she said playfully as she left the room.

Jim turned to Ted and whispered, "What do you mean, tell her?"

Ted smiled. "What! Why not tell her about me?"

"Why don't you just tell her yourself, Mr. Invisible Man with the Magic Mirror? My wife would think I am crazy if I told her that I was talking to a ghost who's been coaching me on leadership principles."

"So you are getting together with Larry tomorrow, huh? Your wife is right. He's very much like you. In all the good and not-so-good ways," Ted said casually.

"Hey, what not-so-good ways?"

"Oh come on, kid! Remember that your poop stinks like everyone else's. Your job as the boy's mentor is to help him grow and learn from your mistakes and avoid making some of the same ones you did."

Jim knew that Ted was right. He was very proud of Larry. He'd hired him when he was just twenty-years old and a sophomore at the university. Larry was doing a summer internship at the company, working in Jim's department. Over the next three years, he worked for Jim during the summer months. Jim offered him a job when he graduated, but Larry wanted to go live in San Diego so he took a position with a company there. Over the years Larry stayed in close contact with Jim, and they had developed a wonderful friendship. To Jim, Larry was like the little brother he never had.

"You were right when you told Marisol that you've had great mentors along the way, Jimmy boy," Ted said, pointing at Jim with the stump of his cigar. "You've also had some good chance givers, haven't you?"

"Yes, I sure have, Ted," Jim admitted. "There have been some people in my career who have given me opportunities to do jobs that were a real stretch for me at the time."

"No doubt about it. But you rose to the challenges and delivered. Most people do just that when given the opportunity and provided the right tutoring along the way."

"Nothing is more important than for leaders to do that, Ted. *Nothing!*" Jim said with passion.

"Well then, how good they are at mentoring should be something they take the time to measure, right?"

"Absolutely. And I don't need a magic mirror to tell me the right questions to ask for that," Jim said confidently.

"Go for it," Ted said, anticipating his pupil's response.

"It's quite simple actually. A leader should ask themselves the following questions:

1. *Are they alert to organizational and people development issues?*
2. *Are they alert to organizational culture issues?*
3. *Do they motivate, inspire, and move others to action?*
4. *Do they look for people to mentor and insist that others do the same?*
5. *Do they give talented people chances and seek stretch assignments for them?*
6. *Do they invest time and money in people development?*
7. *Do they keep people development on the agenda?*
8. *Are they a champion for diversity in their organization?*"

Ted was genuinely impressed with Jim. "Well done, my boy. Well done indeed!"

Jim remained serious. "Nothing is more important than people development. As leaders, if we fall short there we are only hurting our own team."

"And ultimately your legacy as a leader," Ted concluded.

"Without question. The people we develop and help grow will ultimately define our leadership legacy."

Ted gave Jim a smile that told him he was pleased, and then he vanished.

Jim sat in his dimly lit office quietly thinking of the people he had the privilege of mentoring and helping to develop over the years.

The list was not a short one.

CHAPTER 8

The Leader's Balance:
Strategy, Urgency & Risk

The boardroom was especially crowded for the important project review scheduled for that morning. The entire team working on this venture was gathered in the room. They had been working hard on the update presentation. It was without a doubt the most significant undertaking that the company had tackled in many years.

Jim walked in right on time and took his place at the head of the table. He smiled and greeted the team.

"How's everyone doing this morning?" he asked jovially.

There were lots of simultaneous responses. A few moments later – with some folks still serving themselves a cup of coffee from the table at the back of the room – the team leader, David, began speaking.

"Jim," David said, "the team has been working very hard getting ready for this important milestone presentation. We have much to cover this morning, but we think you and the board will be pleased with our progress thus far."

Jim could tell that David was a bit nervous, so he smiled and said, "David, let me just say something very quickly. I have been staying fairly close to what the team has been working on. First, let me say thank you for your hard work! I know this project has consumed many months and has taken much sacrifice from each of you. I've seen many of you here on the weekends. I've read many of the reports, and I know there has been extensive travel to meet with our partners overseas. So thank you for a great team effort. I have no doubt we are headed in the right direction with the project."

Immediately the mood was more relaxed and the team members were smiling. No doubt they were glad to hear their president say those words.

"Thank you, Jim," David said. "We sure do appreciate that. Hopefully you'll still feel that way when we are done with the presentation. There are just a few hurdles that we need to get over yet." As he said that there was some nervous laughter in the room.

"Sounds like you are preparing me for some bad news," Jim said with a broad smile.

"Well, not really bad news, just some opportunities for us." Again there was laughter in the room.

For the next four hours, minus a few coffee breaks, every aspect of the project was discussed. The team covered everything: the R&D status, the operations and manufacturing instrumentation, capacity, training and validation issues, finances, marketing positioning, pricing and competition. No detail was overlooked.

By the end of the meeting there was a sense that the team was headed in the right direction and great progress had been made, but there were still some major obstacles yet to overcome.

After the group reviewed the action items coming from the meeting, Jim thanked the team again.

"Good update, folks," he said sincerely. "You've done a bunch of great work. We still have a way to go, but I have no doubt you will make it happen. I'd like to get back together in one month for another project review. But in the meantime, David, keep me in the loop and let me know if there is anything you need from me. This is the most important project this company is working on, and I want to make sure you have all the support you need from everyone on the staff."

"Thank you, Jim," David said, clearly pleased with his team's effort for the day and with the support the team was getting from the executive staff.

As soon as he got back to his office, Jim saw Ted sitting on his chair with his feet up on his desk. He had a big grin on his face.

Jim closed the door to this office. "Comfy?" he asked.

"Very," Ted replied

"What are you grinning about?" Jim asked as he grabbed a Pepsi from the small refrigerator next to the conference table.

"That meeting you were just in."

"What about it?" Jim asked curiously.

"You did good, kiddo. You showed a great deal of balance," Ted said still grinning.

"Balance? What do you mean?"

"There are three important behaviors that a leader must always keep in balance. First, a good leader keeps focused on strategy and the big picture, but pays attention to the appropriate level of detail," Ted explained.

Jim leaned forward in his chair, taking it all in.

"Second," Ted continued, "a good leader demonstrates a healthy and appropriate sense of urgency. Finally, leaders understand the risks involved in the decision they are making, and they make sure that the team also understands and is aligned with that level of risk."

"I sense some homework coming my way," Jim said.

"Of course you do," Ted chuckled. "What do you think that homework might be?"

Jim smiled knowingly and said, "Mirror, how can I measure my ability to be strategic and focused on the big picture while still maintaining attention to detail?"

The mirror magically appeared and these words became visible:

> *To measure their ability to think strategically and stay focused on the big picture while maintaining attention to detail, leaders should consider:*
>
> 1. *Do they demonstrate an understanding of the business?*
> 2. *How well do they synthesize complex ideas and boil them down into the simple but important points?*
> 3. *How effectively do they translate strategic direction to actionable tactics?*
> 4. *Do they see the broader environment and how it effects the organization and vision?*
> 5. *Do they make global decisions while keeping in mind local or regional considerations?*
> 6. *Do they demonstrate a keen understanding of how all organizational areas function as a unit to drive success?*

"In that meeting today, you demonstrated a very keen sense of this balance between strategy and tactical detail," Ted explained. "It was clear to everyone in the room that you felt comfortable moving from a big picture point of view to a deep level of detail if necessary. Bravo, kid."

Jim was pleased. "Thank you, Ted. I still have work to do to make sure I don't get in the way too much. You know, the engineer in me wants to jump in and try to troubleshoot the technical issues that the R&D team needs to deal with."

"That's good insight for you to keep in mind. But overall I think you do this rather well. You do a nice job pushing the team to make decisions from a global perspective, but you also let the regional teams make their concerns and input heard. That's very important to gain global alignment." Ted paused for a moment, and then said, "Okay, what's the next question to ask the mirror?"

Without hesitation, Jim asked, "Mirror, how do I measure my sense of urgency?"

The screen on the mirror faded and new words came into focus.

To measure their sense of urgency, a leader should:

1.   *Understand the balance between a sense of urgency and sense of "crisis."*

2.   *Determine whether they tend to focus on what's important vs. what's urgent.*

"Number two is easy right? Sometimes things that seem urgent may not be important, Ted explained. "So we should avoid working on things based on their sense of urgency and focus instead on their actual importance."

"Well maybe, but it sure is tempting to spend time on the things that have an urgent feeling to them," Jim confessed. "We probably all do it from time to time."

"Well, you really need to avoid that," Ted said sternly. "For example, a ringing phone seems urgent, so we pick it up as soon as it rings. It feels urgent to us, so we interrupt what we are working on to answer the phone, only to find out that it's just a broker trying to sell us some stock. Just because a phone rings loudly does not mean it's important and has to be answered right now. Make sure you are spending your time wisely."

"Got it," Jim said.

"Number one is probably most important. Remember years ago when we first met and we talked about Soap Opera Players?"

"How could I forget? Some people just like to live in drama all the time."

"Exactly. They want to manage from crisis to crisis. A good question to ask yourself is; *do you feed that culture?*"

Jim thought about it for a few seconds. "I'm afraid maybe I do," he said.

"Not bad, Jimmy boy. You see, that's what looking in the mirror is all about. You don't need anyone to tell you that your style sometimes creates a crisis management environment. You can determine that all by yourself!"

Jim agreed. "I think maybe it's just my Type A personality and hard-charging attitude. Maybe sometimes I act in a way that causes my people to react in fire fighting mode."

"Well, spend some time thinking about that, and then come up with ways to change your words and behavior so that you avoid creating unnecessary crisis. That will allow you more time and energy to manage the actual ones." Ted's advice was right on the money, as usual.

"Okay. Let's talk about risk. Mirror," Jim began, "how should a leader measure their level of risk tolerance and risk taking?"

Once again the words on the mirror faded, and just three seconds later were replaced by this:

> *To measure their level of risk tolerance, leaders should consider the answers to these questions:*
>
> 1. *How willing are they to stand alone on decisions when others disagree?*
> 2. *Do they make prudent decisions based on facts?*
> 3. *How willing are they to make decisions with imperfect information?*
> 4. *How willing are they to change course when new information becomes available?*
> 5. *Do they encourage and reward prudent risk-taking by others?*
> 6. *Do they challenge the status quo and drive change even when it's not popular?*

"I think I do okay in this area. I consider myself a prudent risk taker," Jim said, mostly talking to himself. "I'm quite comfortable making decisions with less than 100% information."

"I agree with you. You get high marks in this area. I am most impressed with your ability to abandon an idea or a project when new data indicates that you should change direction."

"I just don't like throwing good money after bad," Jim said, shrugging his shoulders.

"Well then, why do you think so many leaders and managers have such a hard time killing a project or eliminating a product line when the data clearly indicates that they should?" Ted asked.

Again, Jim shrugged his shoulders. "I don't know. But I know it happens all the time; even here. Maybe I need to model the prudent risk-taking behavior a bit more overtly?"

Jim and Ted looked at each other. Then they both said, "It's not rocket science, it is leadership!"

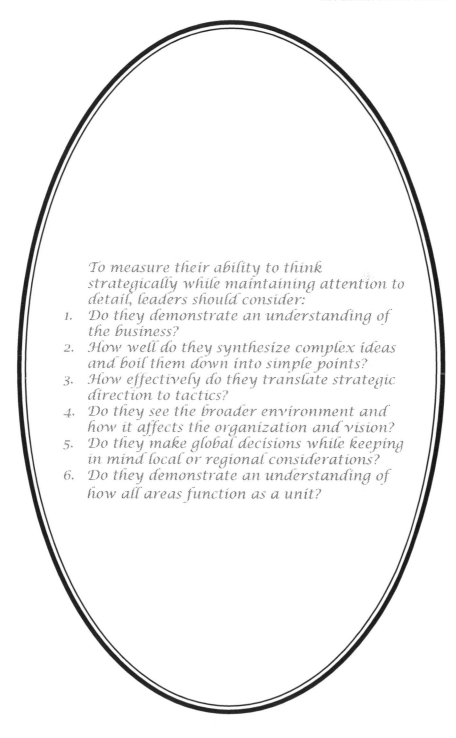

To measure their ability to think strategically while maintaining attention to detail, leaders should consider:

1. *Do they demonstrate an understanding of the business?*
2. *How well do they synthesize complex ideas and boil them down into simple points?*
3. *How effectively do they translate strategic direction to tactics?*
4. *Do they see the broader environment and how it affects the organization and vision?*
5. *Do they make global decisions while keeping in mind local or regional considerations?*
6. *Do they demonstrate an understanding of how all areas function as a unit?*

To measure their sense of urgency, a leader should:

1. Understand the balance between a sense of urgency and sense of "crisis."
2. Determine whether they tend to focus on what's important vs. urgent.

*To measure their level of risk tolerance,
leaders should consider:*

1. *How willing are they to stand alone on
    decisions when others disagree?*
2. *Do they make prudent decisions based
    on facts?*
3. *How willing are they to make decisions
    with imperfect information?*
4. *How willing are they to change
    course when new information becomes
    available?*
5. *Do they encourage and reward
    prudent risk- taking by others?*
6. *Do they challenge the status quo
    and drive change even when it's not
    popular?*

CHAPTER 9

Emotional Intelligence

It was close to 1 a.m. and the only light in the Givens household was coming from the small desk lamp in Jim's study. Jim often enjoyed doing a bit of reading and personal reflection late at night after Marisol was asleep and the house was quiet.

"What are you reading?" Ted asked in an unusually soft voice.

Jim was only slightly startled. He had become used to Ted just popping in. "You know, when I read Goleman's book on emotional intelligence, I thought the concept of EI was a new one."

"Far from it," Ted remarked.

"I see that. From what I'm reading here, the most distant roots of work done on emotional intelligence can be traced back to Darwin's early work on emotional expression for survival and second adaptation," Jim said, reading from his computer screen. "Whatever that means."

"The volume of work done by researchers over the years on EI is impressive," Ted said, sounding like a college professor. "Work done by people like E. L. Thorndike in the early 1920's first defined terms like 'social intelligence' to describe the skill of understanding and managing other people."

"Hey, that's what I just read in Wikipedia," Jim said.

"You know that's one of the least reliable sources of information on the Internet, right?" Ted asked before continuing. "Loads of smart people have influenced the development of the EI concept. For instance, in 1940 David Wechsler described the influence of non-intellective factors on intelligent behavior, and in 1983 Howard Gardner introduced the idea of multiple intelligences. Should I keep going with the history lesson?"

"I have a feeling I know where you are headed with this. I am thinking too hard about it, aren't I? Leave all this psychological stuff to the experts, and as a leader, just focus on how this applies to the real world?"

"Now you are reading my mind! Bottom line is that Goleman boiled it down to a framework to explain the five elements of EI. What are they?"

Jim picked up on his cue and asked, "Mirror, what are Goleman's five elements of emotional intelligence?"

The mirror materialized as usual, although this time it had a special glow as it hovered suspended in midair between Ted and Jim. The words came into focus:

Goleman's five elements of emotional intelligence are self-awareness, self-regulation, motivation, empathy, and social skills.

"What do you say we review each of these?" Ted asked, although he wasn't really giving Jim a choice about it.

"Okay. Let's do them in reverse order just to mix things up."

"Go," Ted said, anticipating his pupil's response.

"Social skills," Jim began. "That's a measure of how well we use influencing abilities such as persuasion, good communication, and listening."

Ted was about to interrupt when Jim put up his hand. "Wait, I'm not done yet," Jim continued. "It's also a measure of how well we negotiate, collaborate and resolve conflict. It relates to things like how well we manage change."

Jim paused. "Are you done now?" Ted asked.

"With that one, yes," Jim answered with a smirk.

"Go on," Ted ordered, disappointed that his student apparently did not need his help at the moment.

"Okay, moving on to empathy. This is a measure of our ability to see other people's points of view, and our ability to behave honestly," Jim said.

Ted waited for a moment and finally broke the silence. "Well, what are you waiting for? Go on!"

"Okay, let's describe the third element of motivation. That's a measure of how much we enjoy challenges. It is also a measure of two other important traits: our ability to take the initiative and our level of optimism."

"Not bad, kid. I see you have been doing your homework."

"The last two are the most important ones for me, starting with self-regulation. It's a measure of how well we control our temper and stress levels. It also considers how we are able to maintain our composure and our ability to think clearly under pressure. Bottom line is that it measures how well we handle impulses and how well we create an environment that nurtures trustworthiness and self-restraint."

"Wow, that's a mouthful!" Ted said.

"I know. That one I've read a few times over. I have a good deal of work to do on that particular element of EI."

"The first step to recovery is admitting you have a problem, my boy. Besides, I know you pretty well. You're not as bad as you think in this area. But it's good that you want to improve on it because it's a critical one if you want to be an effective leader."

Jim nodded. "Now for number one: self-awareness. This examines how our emotions influence our performance. It's a measure of how well we use our values to guide decision-making. It considers how well we do a self-assessment, looking at our strengths and weaknesses and learning from our experiences."

"Seems to me, self-awareness is at the core of what this whole look in the mirror is all about for a leader, right?" Ted asked.

"It sure is. It's also a measure of how self-confident and certain we are about our capabilities, values and goals."

"I'm proud of you, Jimmy. That's good work. Now you know what questions you need to ask yourself. The hard part is answering them."

"That's going to take a few days."

"It might. But don't just answer the questions. Come up with a few specific actions you can take to improve your deficiencies. Of course you should also write down a few things you can do to get better in the areas you are already skilled at," Ted explained.

"I think I'll call it a night," Jim said, yawning.

"One more thing," Ted said. "There are a few more questions that you must ask yourself when thinking about self-awareness. Mirror, what else should a leader consider when evaluating their level of self awareness?"

The mirror's glow grew stronger and soon the words came into view:

When evaluating their level of self-awareness, the leader should ask:

1. *How well do I accept feedback?*
2. *Am I non-defensive when receiving feedback?*
3. *How resilient am I to recover from disappointment?*
4. *Do I recognize my impact on others?*
5. *Do I build effective bridges with colleagues, subordinates, and superiors?*

"Good questions," Jim said.

"Yes they are," Ted agreed. "The final one is one of my favorite qualities of a good leader: their level of intellectual curiosity and ability to learn."

Jim nodded in agreement, and without waiting for Ted to ask first, he turned his attention back to the mirror and said, "Mirror, how can a leader measure their level of intellectual curiosity?"

To measure their level of intellectual curiosity, the leader should ask: Do I...

1. *Demonstrate a desire to keep abreast of current trends?*
2. *Seek to understand emerging technologies?*
3. *Encourage and seek input from experts?*
4. *Encourage others to continue to learn and grow?*
5. *Place a high level of importance on education and training?*

"Okay, I got it. I have a bunch of work to do over the next few days. Now can I go to sleep?"

Just then Marisol appeared in the doorway.

Ted smiled at Jim.

"Hey honey, when are you coming to bed? It's past one in the morning."

"Right now, babe," Jim said as he took his sleepy-eyed wife's hand and walked her back to bed.

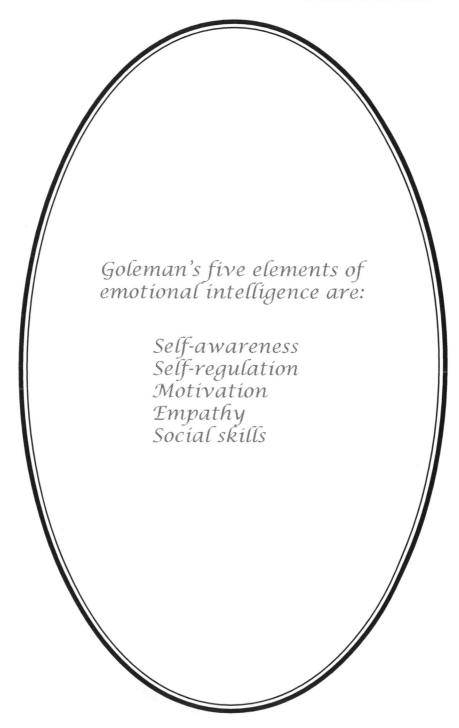

Goleman's five elements of
emotional intelligence are:

Self-awareness
Self-regulation
Motivation
Empathy
Social skills

When evaluating their level of self-awareness, the leader should ask:

1. How well do I accept feedback?
2. Am I non-defensive when receiving feedback?
3. How resilient am I to recover from disappointment?
4. Do I recognize my impact on others?
5. Do I build effective bridges with colleagues, subordinates, and superiors?

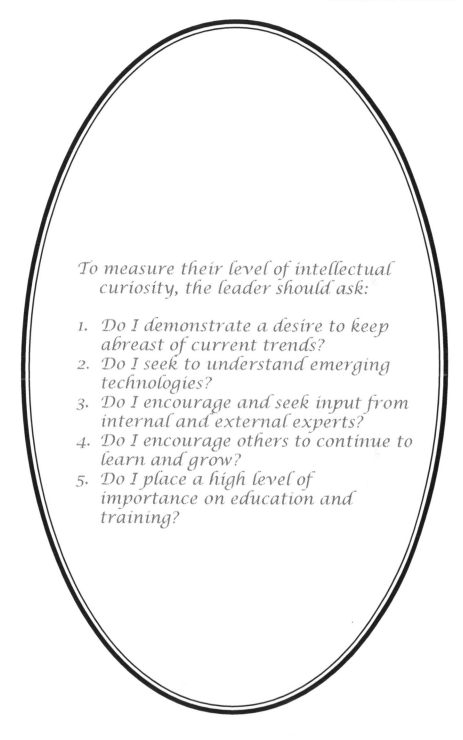

To measure their level of intellectual curiosity, the leader should ask:

1. Do I demonstrate a desire to keep abreast of current trends?
2. Do I seek to understand emerging technologies?
3. Do I encourage and seek input from internal and external experts?
4. Do I encourage others to continue to learn and grow?
5. Do I place a high level of importance on education and training?

CHAPTER 10

Cultural Intelligence

Morning came quickly.

"Daddy, Mommy said you have to get up now," Michelle whispered in Jim's ear.

Jim opened one eye and was greeted by his daughter's smile. "Good morning, sweetheart. How are you this morning?"

"Fine. But Mommy said you need to get out of bed *now*," she insisted.

"Okay, sweetie. Tell Mommy that Daddy will be down in ten minutes. I just need to wash up."

Michelle ran out of the room screaming the whole way down the stairs to the kitchen, "Mommy, Daddy said he'll be down in the ten minutes!"

It took him more like fifteen minutes, but Jim finally made his way to the kitchen.

"Good morning, babe," Marisol said with a warm smile. "You told me to wake you up early today to get to the yard work."

"Yeah, I know."

"It's landscaping day," Michelle said with her mouth full of pancakes.

"Don't talk with your mouth full, please," Marisol said gently. "Besides, I don't think Daddy is as excited as you and me about landscaping day."

"I am too excited," Jim said a bit defensively. "I'm just a bit tired, that's all."

"What kept you so late last night," Marisol asked.

"I think it was Mr. Ted," Michelle whispered so her mom would not hear.

"Just doing more work on the self-assessment I told you about last week," Jim said quickly, to deflect from Michelle's comment.

"You're really working hard on that assessment," Marisol said. "That's great. What aspects are you looking at now?"

"Emotional intelligence," Jim said casually as he sipped his coffee.

"Goleman's EI?" Marisol asked.

"That's the one," Jim answered.

"I like that book," Marisol said. "It was centered on self-reflection, motivation, empathy and social awareness or something like that?"

"That's pretty close," Jim said, impressed that Marisol remembered so much. It had been years since they read Goleman's book. "It was actually self-awareness rather than self-reflection. But you've got the idea."

"For me there was always one part missing when it came to the whole emotional intelligence thing," Marisol said.

"What's that?" Jim asked.

"Our individual cultural intelligence index," she replied.

Jim and Marisol had spoken of this in the past.

"You know what? You are absolutely right. That's a good thing for leaders to measure themselves against," Jim remarked.

"Absolutely," Marisol agreed. "Adapting your personal style to each unique situation and being comfortable in different environments are critical for any leader's success – but especially for those working in a global environment like you do."

Jim nodded.

"You should talk to Jeannie about it. She's teaching a class on EI and CI at the university. They finally added it to the business school curriculum," Marisol said. "In fact, she wrote an article on it and gave me a draft. Let me get it for you."

Marisol went to the study and searched through her briefcase. "Found it!" she hollered, and began reading the paper as she walked back into the kitchen. "Here's how she defines cultural intelligence:"

Cultural intelligence (CI) is your capability to grow personally through continuous learning and good understanding of diverse cultural heritage, wisdom and values, and to deal effectively with people from different cultural backgrounds and levels of understanding.

Marisol quickly scanned the rest of the document. "Why is CI important," she continued. "Listen to what she writes:"

> *Cultural intelligence is a new domain of intelligence that has immense relevance to the increasingly global and diverse workplace. Some aspects of culture are easy to see – the obvious things like art and music and behavior. However, the significant and most challenging parts of other cultures are hidden. These include beliefs, values, expectations, attitudes, and assumptions.*
>
> *Cultural intelligence will help you manage effectively across cultural differences, in particular:*
> 1. *Cultural intelligence lowers the cultural barriers caused by 'us' and 'them' and to allows you to predict what 'they' are thinking and how 'they' will react to your behavior patterns.*
> 2. *Having cultural intelligence allows you to harness the power of cultural diversity.*
>
> *In today's globalizing world, cultural intelligence is an important and necessary tool for every leader who deals with diverse and global teams of employees, customers, partners, competitors, governments, and other business partners.*

Just then Jim heard Ted's voice. "Listen to the lady; she's smarter than you and I both combined."

Jim smiled.

"What are you smiling at?" Marisol asked.

"Nothing, darling. Tell me this. What would be the best way to measure myself on cultural intelligence?"

Marisol thought for a moment as she sipped her coffee. "If I were you, I guess I would ask myself a few questions. First, how comfortable am I when I am among a group of people who are of a different ethnic background? Second, when visiting a foreign country, how well do I adapt to the cultural norms?"

"Do you mean, do I try to sample their foods and involve myself in their customs?" Jim asked for clarification.

"Yes. And are you curious about their customs and traditions? Do you ask questions to indicate a genuine interest in their customs? Third, do you get frustrated when speaking with people with accents, or do you work extra hard to understand what they are saying and even try to communicate in their native language when possible?"

"Hard to do for a guy who only speaks English," Jim said. "Americans are the only ones who think everyone else should speak their language."

Marisol smiled because she and her husband had talked about language issues many times before. "You've learned a bit of Spanish from being with my family," she said proudly.

"I know, but not well enough to speak it in meetings when I go to Mexico," Jim confessed.

"Well, dear, that is something you could have and should have done something about already. I think every executive should try to speak at least two if not three or four languages. If nothing else it demonstrates their willingness to learn and adapt to other cultures, and it might encourage their people to do the same."

"That's a great point, babe," Jim said with genuine admiration for his wife.

"So that's another question to ask: have I learned to speak another language well enough to communicate with others in their native tongue?"

"These are very helpful, Marisol. I'll definitely add them to the long list of questions on EI that I already have to ask myself."

"Don't forget to add a few more, like: how thoroughly do I sponsor the diversity process in my organization? Do I make diversity an important part of my team's agenda? Am I holding myself and others accountable for fostering an organizational culture in which diversity is appreciated and maximized?"

Marisol knew what she was talking about. Her work as a civil rights attorney made her an expert in the field of diversity.

"Wow, hang on! I should be writing these down," Jim said enthusiastically.

"I tell you what I will do for you, dear. You get going on the mulch, and I'll write these down for you. How does that sound?" Marisol said with a huge grin.

"Okay, I got it," Jim said. He wasn't looking forward to pushing fourteen yards of mulch around the lawn. Now he wished he had agreed to the landscaper's price to do the work. "Can I have some pancakes first?"

"Of course," Marisol said, kissing him on the forehead.

Ted materialized in the seat next to Michelle. "Your mommy is one smart lady! Maybe that's why you are so smart, too. You sure didn't get that from your daddy."

Michelle giggled.

"And you're pretty, too. You *definitely* did not get *that* from your daddy."

This time Michelle laughed out loud.

"What so funny, cupcake?" Marisol asked Michelle. Jim smiled at Michelle, cocked his head to one side and raised his eyebrows.

"It's our secret, Mommy," Jim said for Michelle, who continued to giggle, covering her mouth with her hands.

"You have lots of work to do, Jimmy boy," Ted growled. "Starting with the landscaping, and then with your EI and CI assessments."

Jim sighed.

Ted winked, waved Michelle a good-bye kiss, and disappeared in a shower of multicolored sparkles.

Ten hours later, Jim, exhausted from a long hard day of work, was actually feeling quite satisfied. Sometimes just doing mindless manual labor was therapeutic for him.

He had already put Michelle down to bed, and as he sat at his desk in the study he notice the note from Marisol. As promised at breakfast, she had written down the questions on cultural intelligence. Her penmanship was flawless. The note said:

To measure your cultural awareness index, ask yourself the following questions:

1. *How comfortable am I when I am among a group of people who are of a different ethnic background?*
2. *When visiting a foreign country, how well do I adapt to the cultural norms?*
3. *Am I curious about other people's customs and traditions? Do I ask questions to indicate a genuine interest in their way of life?*
4. *Do I get frustrated when speaking with people who have accents, or do I work extra hard to understand what they are saying — even trying to communicate in their native language whenever possible?*
5. *Have I learned to speak another language well enough to communicate with others in their native language?*
6. *Do I make diversity an important part of my team's agenda?*
7. *Am I holding myself and others accountable for fostering an organizational culture in which diversity is appreciated and maximized?*

I love you, M

P.S. I think you have a very high CI index!

CHAPTER 11

Team Builder and Innovator

It was very quiet in the aircraft's business class cabin. The flight attendants had finished their meal service, and most people had reclined their seats, donned their sleep masks and settled in for the long flight to Japan.

Jim had booked a coach ticket for the lengthy journey, but had been fortunate enough to get an upgrade to business class thanks to his frequent flyer status with American Airlines. He felt it was important to set an example of cost-consciousness for his team, so he always traveled coach rather than spending extra for business or first class tickets.

Jim always had trouble sleeping in airplanes, so he usually had a bite to eat and watched a movie while he worked on his e-mail. Once he had sufficiently exhausted himself, he then tried to get a few hours of sleep. They were never very restful hours, but at least he could function when he landed.

Jim had just finished eating and was watching the in-flight movie when suddenly the screen went blank and a new image appeared. Jim immediately recognized the scene.

"Okay, Ted," Jim hissed. "I know you're in here."

Ted materialized in the empty aisle seat next to Jim.

"I knew it was too good to be true that I would have an empty seat next to me all the way to Japan," Jim said, rolling his eyes.

"What! Not happy to see me?" Ted asked with his usual sarcasm.

"No, I am always happy to see you. I just thought that I would have a quiet and peaceful trip to Japan, that's all."

"And waste fourteen hours? I don't think so, buddy boy. Recognize the scene on the video?"

Jim quickly turned his attention to the small screen in front of him. "I sure do," he said with a gentle smile. "Those were some good days!"

"How old were you then?" Ted asked, although he already knew the answer.

"I must have been in my early thirties," Jim said, searching his memory.

"Thirty-three," Ted said smugly. "Tell me about the team and the project you were working on."

"The team was the best, and the project was the most challenging and entertaining I've ever had the pleasure of leading," Jim said without hesitation.

"What made it so much fun?"

"This was the first time that the company had really engaged a true cross-functional and global team to get after this new product development and introduction," Jim began. "The key to the team's success was the fact that everyone was committed to the end goal, and we also had total support from the most senior levels of the organization."

"What else made it so much fun?"

"We had great freedom to operate, and we had the resources we needed to get the job done," Jim continued. "Also, we created an environment in which it was not only okay to take risks, but it was necessary and expected."

Ted smiled knowingly. "Keep going."

"Well, let's see. We also tapped into everyone's expertise and really considered their personal styles to make sure that we got the most out of everyone involved," Jim added.

"You did indeed," Ted said. "Why in the heck is that so hard to recreate in other teams?"

"That, sir, is the ten million dollar question," Jim replied, hoping that Ted had the answer.

"You know the answer as well as I do, Jimbo."

"I guess so," Jim admitted. "I've been trying to recreate the success of that team ever since, and to be honest, I've never been able to completely pull it off."

Ted nodded in agreement. "You're right. Most teams are not as effective or as successful as that one. Everything about that team was just right. The right people, with the right leaders, in the right environment – all those elements conspired to make you guys successful."

"So what are you saying? It was the perfect storm and can never be repeated?" Jim asked.

"I did not say that!" Ted insisted. "But it takes hard work and a focus on the key dynamics that drive team innovation."

"Breakthrough thinking," Jim said to himself, recalling a lesson Ted had shared with him some time ago about how leaders behave to drive innovation in teams.

"Breakthrough thinking indeed," Ted said. "So instead of sitting here watching another silly movie or playing with your e-mail, re-read *Breakthrough Thinking: The Legacy Leader's Role In Driving Innovation* and refresh your memory on what leaders must do to make it happen!"

As Ted said those words, a copy of the book materialized on Jim's tray table.

"Well, this should put me to sleep," Jim mumbled.

"What's that?"

"Oh, nothing. I can't wait to read it again," Jim replied.

"I thought you would feel that way about it. We'll talk in a few hours," Ted said. He reclined his seat, put on his noise reduction headset, and dozed off to sleep.

Two hours passed quickly as Jim read through most of the book.

Suddenly his thoughts were interrupted by the sound of Ted's voice.

"Well, was it worth a second look?" Ted asked.

Jim hated to admit it, but Ted was right as usual. "Yes it was," he said. "It really is amazing how we miss doing the simple things that drive team innovation."

"What struck you the most?"

Jim thought for a moment. "I guess I really need to remind myself of the importance of the leader's role in moving the team through the stages of breakthrough thinking."

Jim paused again, and then added, "I was also reminded of something I've known for more than twenty years about the stages of forming, norming, storming, and performing, and what I must keep in mind to move a team from one stage to the next."

"Kid, if a team is not performing at peak effectiveness and accomplishing great things, its leader need not look any further than in the mirror to ask a few simple questions."

Jim smiled. "I guess that's my cue?"

Ted raised one eyebrow and asked, "Well, what do you think?"

Jim settled back in his seat. "Mirror," he said, "how should leaders measure their ability to build teams and drive innovation?"

The mirror magically appeared and began to sparkle as the words came into clear focus.

To measure their effectiveness as team builders and innovation drivers, leaders should ask themselves:

1. *How effectively have they communicated the team's vision and objectives?*

2. *Do they create diverse teams in which diversity of thought is not only expected, but encouraged?*
3. *Do they demonstrate an understanding of team stages and the leader's role in each of these stages?*
4. *Do they model the right leadership behaviors that encourage and drive team innovation?*
5. *Do they use power and influence prudently and in a non-intimidating way?*
6. *Do they recognize and reward teams and team members appropriately?*

Ted and Jim both studied the words on the mirror.

Jim broke the silence. "These may seem like simple questions, but they are much more complex than they appear."

"Maybe so, but you do have some data to rely on, don't you?"

"I guess so. We can simply look at how successful teams have been in delivering the results they initially set out to accomplish," Jim said, thinking out loud.

"Truth is that most teams fall a bit short of hitting all their objectives. Or they are delayed in getting them done, or they are over budget, or yada yada yada," Ted said. "Now before you jump all over me, I'm not saying that means that these teams are slackers or are not doing good work. All I am suggesting is that they could be even more effective and innovative if the environment was more conducive to breakthrough thinking."

"I agree with you, Ted. So what you are saying is that measuring results in this area is pretty straightforward, like black and white. We can see when the teams are working effectively and when they are not."

"That's almost always true," Ted agreed.

"But consider this: how do you know if you have been effective in communicating the vision? I mean, that's rather subjective."

"Is it really? Maybe it's as simple as asking the team members when you see them in the hallway to tell you what the team's vision and objectives are. If you do that a few times, you'll know pretty quickly how effective you've been at communicating the vision and objectives."

Jim thought about Ted's advice. "You're talking about the way Henry used to do it, aren't you?"

Henry had been the plant manager in ITA's Brazil manufacturing location until his retirement three years ago. Henry was known for stopping folks in the hallways or in the cafeteria and asking them to recite the plant's mission and key objectives.

Henry made it fun for them and recited the company's vision with them so as not to intimidate anyone. He always did it good-naturedly, but if someone did not know what the vision was, he would tell them to memorize it because he was going to ask them again a few days later. After a while, everyone in the plant knew what the vision and objectives were.

During a company party at the plant about two years after he retired, Henry was asked to say a few words. He stood at the microphone and asked the audience, "What is this plant's mission?"

The audience recited the short mission statement in unison, and at the end they all applauded and cheered.

"Henry got it," Ted said. "Do you think he ever doubted whether or not he was effective in communicating the vision and objectives?"

"I see your point."

"Jimmy, each of these questions is important to answer, and one of the best ways to answer them is to think of examples in which you've either done it well or you've done it poorly. You can also think of examples you've witnessed of someone else doing it well. Then think about what you can do to make sure that the next time you have the opportunity to make it right, you do just that."

Jim nodded intently.

"Doing a self-evaluation is not easy work," Ted continued. "It can seem subjective if all you do is look at the questions and give them a yes or no answer. But that would cause you to miss the point completely!"

"That makes sense to me. If I turn these questions into reminders of how to behave and not just a review of how I've behaved in the past, I can more effectively impact my team's future."

Ted and Jim starred at each other for a few seconds. Then they both smiled.

"Hey, that was quite deep," Jim said with a coy smile. "I should write that down."

"I will admit that was pretty darn insightful," Ted said with a hint of admiration for his pupil.

"Wow! A compliment from you, Ted?" Jim asked as he patted himself on the back.

"Don't let it go to your head, kid. Everybody gets lucky once in a while. Anyway, you've got some work to do, so get to it," Ted ordered.

"It will have to wait until the trip back from Japan. I'll have lots of hours on the way home to give it some thought. Right now I am going to get some sleep!" Jim reclined his seat as far back as it would go.

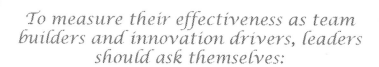

To measure their effectiveness as team builders and innovation drivers, leaders should ask themselves:

1. *How effectively have they communicated the team's vision?*
2. *Do they create diverse teams?*
3. *Do they understand their role in managing team stages?*
4. *Do they model the right leadership behaviors that encourage and drive team innovation?*
5. *Do they use power and influence in a non-intimidating way?*
6. *Do they recognize and reward teams and team members appropriately?*

CHAPTER 12

Leveraging Style

Jim was sitting in the back of the conference room listening to Brian as he introduced the concept of "Insight Discoveries" for a large group of ITA managers and directors. Brian, a trained Insights consultant, had already completed a two-day training with Jim's executive team a few weeks earlier.

It was not the first time that Jim had experienced the Insights training module. He was first introduced to the concept a few years earlier when he attended a weeklong executive development program. He was so impressed with it that as President he made it mandatory training for every manager and director in the company. His plan was to eventually have a few folks on the HR team become trainers in the process so that they could then roll out the Insights concept to every professional in the company at all levels.

Ted materialized next to Jim.

"What is it about this Insights thing that you like so much?" he asked with a whisper, despite the fact that no one else could hear or see him.

Jim leaned toward him and, trying to speak without moving his lips, said, "It's a very effective way of getting to know your style and the style of others."

"Hey, that's pretty good! Your lips didn't move at all," Ted said with a chuckle.

"Thanks. You know what I always say – if you're going to pretend to be a ventriloquist, it helps to have a big dummy by your side," Jim quipped.

"Oh, hardy har har," Ted sneered.

Just then Jim's administrative assistant quietly slipped into the conference room and motioned to get his attention. Jim collected his notebook and his Blackberry phone and met her in the hallway.

"You have an urgent call from France," she said.

"Is it Richard?" he asked as they both walked quickly back to Jim's office.

"Yes, Richard is on, along with a few others. They are holding on a conference line and said they really need to speak with you right away."

"I have a feeling I know what this is about. If it is, I'm going to need you to find Kim for me. Is she in today?"

"I saw her this morning," she answered.

"I'll let you know if I need her, thanks."

Jim hit the speaker button on his phone. "Good afternoon, all," Jim said cheerfully, taking into account the time difference for the folks on the phone.

"Hi Jim. This is Richard. Sorry to bug you, but we have a rather urgent matter to discuss with you," he said in his usual serious tone. He's a typical 'blue,' Jim thought to himself. Richard was the VP of International Operations.

"No problem, Richard. Who else is there with you?"

"We've got Francis, Hans, BJ, Lorenz and Yuki here in Lyon," Richard replied.

They each took turns saying hello.

As he heard the names, Jim was thinking, 'blue', 'red', 'green', 'yellow', and 'blue'. Jim knew each of them personally and quite well. Francis was the head of QA in the Lyon office. Hans was Director of Manufacturing, also in Lyon. BJ was the European Director of Sales. Lorenz and Yuki were both Marketing Directors: Lorenz for Europe and Yuki for the Asia Pacific region.

By the time Jim spoke again, Ted was already sitting comfortably on the office couch.

"Hello, everyone. Good to hear your voices. I suspect the subject is the launch of the new Trident?"

"Yes it is, Jim." Richard's voice betrayed his feelings about the project. He had already told Jim that he was frustrated with the lack of data the marketing team had compiled to support the product launch.

"Okay. Let me get Kim in here with me because I think she will be able to contribute to the discussion."

Just as he finished saying those words, Kim cracked Jim's office door open and said, "I hear you may be looking for me?"

"Yes, Kim, come on in. We have Richard, Francis, Hans, BJ, Lorenz and Yuki on the phone," he said.

Kim smiled and greeted everyone individually.

"Kim is a perfect 'orange,'" Ted said. "She's got that 'fiery red' style with a strong 'sunshine yellow' undertone."

Jim nodded in agreement with Ted's comment.

For the next forty five minutes there was a lively discussion on the Trident product launch. Jim facilitated the discussion more than anything else, relying heavily on his understanding of each leader's style to keep the dialogue positive and on track.

The 'cool blue' leaders wanted specific data to support marketing's forecast. Neither of them liked surprises and both were uncomfortable with the unpredictability of the marketplace. The 'earthy green' leader wanted to make sure that all opinions were heard and that relationships were not being bruised in the process of deciding what to do.

The 'sunshine yellow' leader wanted the team to be more spontaneous and flexible. He argued that the team could adjust the forecast on the fly if necessary, while the 'fiery red' leaders – including Jim – became a bit irritated with the inefficiency of the meeting and wanted to move the team swiftly toward decisions and a conclusion.

Ted enjoyed the entire meeting, often making comments that only Jim could hear and react to. Finally the conference call was concluded; a few decisions had been reached and most were satisfied with the progress they had made.

"Let's get back together Friday morning this week and see where we are with the follow-ups we discussed. We will make whatever final decisions are still pending at that point," Jim said.

"Sounds good," Richard said on behalf of all the participants at his end.

"Great. I appreciate the work all of you are doing on this, folks," Jim said. "We may not make perfect decisions, but we will make the best ones we can with the information we have. I am sure of that."

Everyone said goodbye and the call finally ended. Kim and Jim spoke for a few more minutes and then she was off to her next meeting.

"That was a perfect example of why it is so important for leaders to know their own style and understand the styles of others," Ted said with a smile. He had clearly found the meeting entertaining.

"Boy, you got that right!" Jim agreed. "That's why I want everyone here to go through the Insights training program. I was skeptical at first, but I am now convinced that some of it works quite well."

"It certainly does," Ted insisted. "As with anything else, there is no need to overcomplicate things. Nevertheless, having a basic understanding of those four simple styles – the red, blue, green and yellow – along with their likes and dislikes, helps to make communications a whole lot easier."

"It goes beyond just understanding their likes and dislikes," Jim added. "The program provides insight into how to present ideas so that they are more appealing to people, which creates a more effective work environment."

"When you get good at recognizing people's styles and you are able to adapt your own style to communicate with them, the world turns into a much nicer place for everybody," Ted said, puffing on his smokeless cigar and gazing pensively into middle space.

"Gosh, that sounded almost poetic, Ted," Jim said. "I didn't know you were so... sensitive."

Ted ignored Jim's comment. "So how should leaders measure themselves against their ability to read and manage people's styles? Importantly, how should they measure themselves against their ability to manage their *own* style?"

"Those are great questions, All Wise One," Jim said with feigned reverence.

"Whatever, Beavis. Just get the answer for me, would you?"

Jim wiped the smile from his face and cleared his throat. "Mirror, how should leaders measure their effectiveness in reading and managing people's unique styles?"

As usual, the mirror materialized and immediately went to work responding to Jim's question:

To measure their effectiveness in reading and managing personality styles, leaders should consider the following questions:

1. *Do they remain aware of their personal style preferences and adjust them to the situation?*
2. *Do they consider other people's personal styles and adjust theirs to more effectively communicate with them?*
3. *Do they read and consider other people's body language and adjust theirs accordingly?*
4. *Do they understand the different personality styles and how to influence them?*

Jim read the words out loud. Ted listened with uncharacteristic patience.

"You know what?" Jim asked rhetorically. "These may be too vague to be effective questions. Unless..."

"Unless what?" Ted insisted.

"The bottom line here is that this is as 'touchy feely' as one can get. I mean, there is a whole science of psychology that attempts to understand human behavior and predict it accurately."

"No doubt about that," Ted agreed. "Also try to predict behavior when people are under pressure or stress. They can become different people altogether."

"Right. There are many different ways to categorize style. So what is most important is that everyone on the team shares a common language and understanding of the styles."

"Keep going, you're on the right track."

"What I must do as a leader is to make sure that we have a common understanding of the various types of styles. This will help put everyone on a level playing field. Second, if we each understand what our own individual style is, in whatever system we choose, we will be able to articulate what our preferences are."

"Go on," Ted said, encouraging Jim to draw the logical conclusion.

"Third, if each of us has a basic understanding of our individual style and we understand what the other person's style is, we should be able to better communicate with one another."

"Wow, that's a mouthful. But it makes sense. More importantly, if you follow that simple logic, then the questions that the mirror has posed to you do make sense, don't they?"

"Yes they do," Jim agreed.

Jim reflected for a while, and then thought out loud, "having my team go through the Insights training is really a good idea."

"Whether Insights or some other model, the important thing is that you are all on the same page in terms of understanding basic styles and how to best communicate and influence people who exhibit those styles," Ted said.

"If a leader does that effectively, they win."

To measure their effectiveness in reading and managing personality styles, leaders should consider the following questions:

1. *Do they remain aware of their personal style preferences and adjust them to the situation?*
2. *Do they consider other people's personal styles and adjust theirs to more effectively communicate with them?*
3. *Do they read and consider other people's body language and adjust theirs accordingly?*
4. *Do they understand the different personality styles and how to influence them?*

CHAPTER 13

The Leadership Journey

Six months later

Jim was sitting quietly in his study. For a moment he was mesmerized by the beauty of the trees in his backyard. He was admiring the blazing colors of the leaves. A gentle wind was blowing, and leaves where floating away from their branches. Autumn was back.

It had been nearly six months since Ted had reappeared in Jim's life and since he had begun working on his self- assessment. Jim realized that this would not be a one-time deal. He had already decided his leadership journey would include an ongoing "look in the mirror" to take stock of how he was doing as a leader.

Jim figured that if he tackled one or two of the assessment areas each month, it would take him about six months to complete the cycle. Then he could repeat the process. He knew it would take some discipline, but he was committed to keeping his leadership skills sharp.

Suddenly Jim's computer beeped, indicating the arrival of a message. He saw that it was from his good friend, Chester. He was always happy to get a message from Chester Elton. Chester always had a smile on his face, and nothing but positive words came from his mouth. Jim had really enjoyed getting to know him over the past few years.

It was amazing to Jim that despite his incredible success as a bestselling author, popular speaker and world-renowned employee recognition guru, Chester remained humble and down to earth.

Jim quickly opened Chester's e-mail and read it.

Hi Jim:

It was great to speak with you last week! I am so glad things are going well for you in your new role. You will do great things for ITA! Hey, I think you will enjoy this poem. It was written by my grandfather, David Horton Elton (well that's the way he tells it anyway… although the real author, Dale Wimbrow, may have something to say about that! ☺) Since you've been working on your leader's critical self-assessment and taking a look at "the man in the mirror," I thought you would find it appropriate. Enjoy! Chester

The Guy in the Glass

When you've got all you want in your struggle for pelf,
And the world crowns you King for a day,
Then go to the mirror and look at yourself,
And see what that guy has to say.
For it isn't your Father or Mother or Wife,
Who judgment upon you must pass.
The feller whose verdict counts most in your life,
Is the guy staring back from the glass.
He's the feller to please, never mind all the rest,
For he's with you clear up to the end,
And you've passed your most dangerous, difficult test
If the guy in the glass is your friend.
You may be like Jack Horner and chisel a plum,
And think you're a wonderful guy,
But the man in the glass says you're only a bum
If you can't look him straight in the eye.
You can fool the whole world down the pathway of years,
And get pats on the back as you pass.
But your final reward will be heartaches and tears,
If you cheated the guy in the glass.

Ted was quietly reading the message over Jim's shoulder. "Those words ring true, don't they?"

"They sure do, Ted," Jim said with a sigh. "You know, the older I get, the more my sense of urgency increases."

"Your sense of urgency?" Ted asked.

"I have a sense of urgency to make sure that I am doing something worthwhile. Life is short, and it moves very fast. In a blink of the eye, I'm forty-eight years old. Well, I just want to make sure I am doing something worthwhile."

"Jimmy, think of our good friend, Charlie Garcia. How does he define success?"

"Finding and being true to your passion."

"That's a good way of thinking, my boy. Leadership is your passion. It always has been. You are good at it. And you are using your God-given talent as a leader to create a better world for those you care for the most."

"Listen to him, sweetheart."

Jim looked up, startled to see a smiling Marisol standing in the doorway.

"So how long have you known?" he asked.

"About Mr. Ted? Oh, I've known for a little while," she said coyly.

"Michelle told, didn't she?"

"Of course, darling. How long do you think an eight year old can keep a…"

Ted interrupted, "Wait, wait! Go back to what you said when you first came in, Marisol. It was really good advice and I don't want the wise guy here to miss it."

"What? About Jim listening to you?" she asked, smiling broadly.

"That's it!" Ted said, slapping Jim's back. "Listen to me, boy."

"I'm listening. I'm listening," Jim insisted.

"You're on a leadership journey, Jimmy," Ted said. "Part of your journey includes making mistakes and learning from them. That's why an ongoing self-assessment is so important."

Jim nodded.

"It's good that you have a sense of urgency about doing something worthwhile," Ted said. "You want to know one way you can determine what's worth accomplishing? It can be defined with one word, Jimmy."

"Legacy," Jim said.

"That's right. You want to know what never gets carved on a tombstone? The words CEO, President, or Director of this or that. So, you want another way of thinking about what is worthwhile? Ask yourself this question: what is the purpose of my leadership journey?"

"To create a legacy that I and those I love can be proud of," Jim answered.

"To create a legacy you and those who love you can be proud of," Ted repeated. "And son, you are doing just that. You are a man of character and integrity, a good husband and father, a loyal friend and servant leader who puts the interests of his followers before his own. Now *those* are words worth carving on a tombstone. I am proud of you."

Jim turned to Marisol who smiled and nodded, her eyes dewy with tears.

Her expression told Jim that she wholeheartedly agreed with Ted.

SECTION TWO

The Leader's Lobotomy
2nd Edition

The Leader's Lobotomy

A Fable
2nd Edition

The Legacy Leader
Avoids Promotion-Induced Amnesia

Anthony López

Foreword by Chester Elton

PRAISE FOR
The Leader In the Mirror

"Put The Legacy Leader Series of Books *on your must-read list. Tony brings fundamental leadership concepts into focus in a straightforward and practical way."*
Buster Houchins
Vice Chairman
CTPartners

"Tony brings every leader, no matter how new or seasoned, back to the basics of Leadership. As Leaders we must intentionally demonstrate these basics to assure we have a loyal followership that achieves results and moves our organizations forward to success. Thank you for helping me 'look in the mirror' and reminding me it is my responsibility to practice all of the antidotes and learn the lessons to prevent PIA."
Joy Schreder
Vice President
Great Lakes, State Farm

"The Legacy Leader strikes again! Tony has a way of getting to the heart of leadership fundamentals and making them practical! A must read for all Leaders!"
Melanie Barstad
President, Women's Health Initiatives (retired)
Johnson & Johnson

"The message of this humorous book really hits the mark. These simple concepts must be mastered by all successful leaders."
Richard Sofinowski
Retired Johnson & Johnson Executive

"The Leader's Lobotomy delivers the goods. The storytelling draws you in and quickly reminds you of critical lessons that every senior executive must remember to be an effective leader."

Lynn Hanessian
CEO
Zeno Group

"I found myself laughing as I read the story, until I realized how true to corporate life it really is! Every leader must keep in mind the fundamental concepts brought to life in this engaging story."
Eric J. Guerin, CPA, MBA
Finance Director
New Business Development and R&D
ETHICON, Inc.

"Timeless advice. Tony takes a whimsical approach to reminding us what we all learned, then forgot, as we advanced in our careers. It's not inevitable if we don't want it to be. The basics will never go out of style."
Thomas A. Barbolt, Ph.D., D.A.B.T.
Distinguished Research Fellow
ETHICON, Inc.

"In Good to Great, *Jim Collins coached us all to stop looking at the mirror of our own self-accomplishment and look out the window at all the people who have made our experience possible. Tony López teaches us how to look out the window, see the others who have contributed greatly to our life, and pass on the opportunities to those we are privileged to lead. Thank you, Tony."*
Rick Hawks
Senior Pastor
The Chapel, Fort Wayne

"Superb writing with a compelling message makes The Leader's Lobotomy an instant classic. Once again Tony reminds us that leadership is an ongoing journey which redefines each of us as we go along. Forgetting the past and what we learn from it is a sure way to repeat the same mistakes in the future. Lead, follow, or get out of the way!"
Ivan Tornos
Vice President & General Manager
Covidien, Latin America & Canada

"Every leader must read this book! Having been a leader in both the private and public sectors, sometimes I've found myself starting to get this disease; but there is always a 'Ted' in our lives to remind us of the importance of not forgetting where we came from, and the importance of keeping our beliefs and values top priority. It's a 1-2-3 methodology to avoid forgetting the principles of assertiveness, good communication, empathy and purpose. In a funny and easy read book, Tony captured it all. I loved it!"
Aixa G. López-Santiago, P.E.
Business Development & Marketing Director
McNally Engineering, LLC

"You surely know a leader afflicted by Promotion-Induced Amnesia (PIA). They are the ones that forgot everything they knew about leadership when they got that new title. You are not alone. This chronic and debilitating condition affects leaders in organizations around the world. This book provides the fundamental principles you need to prevent the onset of PIA. If you are already suffering from PIA, don't despair, Tony has the antidote for your ailment! Take it along on your next airplane ride! I did, and could not put it down."
Dan R. Matlis
President
Axendia

"A very practical approach to more effective leadership. When applied well, the result will foster a more creative and productive environment for all those who depend upon that leader. Such an environment can only help individuals and businesses overcome the many and varied challenges confronting them today and tomorrow."
Richard Johnson
Director, Regulatory Compliance
DePuy, Johnson & Johnson

"Ted is the man (or is it angel?)! Leaders who listen to him can, and do, lead. All in leadership positions should read The Leader's Lobotomy *while standing in front of a mirror and looking at themselves; picture their actions, and see and listen to their CGA."*
Donald Bowers
Community Builder
Regional Director, NYC/NJ FIRST Robotics

In a novel fashion, Tony has delivered management concepts that must be learned and used by novice managers, and that must be remembered by veteran leaders who may be in need of refocusing.
Jesse Penn
Former President
Cordis Inc.

"Leaders who view their contribution in terms of legacy – and not just the here and now – are the authentic ones. They tend to exhibit greater integrity of purpose, for they wish to be stewards of something greater than themselves. Tony López is one of the few thought leaders today driving this message. This is what draws me to his body of work."
John Fayad
Publisher
Business Book Review

DEDICATION

To Cristina and Marisa.
You are my legacy. You are my life.
I'm proud to be your father and
I love you both – Dad

ACKNOWLEDGEMENTS

Over the past twenty years I have had the great fortune of being associated with wonderful people in both my personal and professional lives. Many have influenced and shaped my thinking. I've learned much from family members, friends, and colleagues over the years. It's impossible to acknowledge everyone, as I will surely miss some who have had a positive impact in helping me become the person that I am today. I am eternally grateful to all.

To Thomas Barbolt, Aixa López, Daniel Matlis, Tania Maldonado, and especially my better half, Yvette, thank you for patiently reading the manuscript - in some cases more than once - and helping to edit the work of a writer who can only be labeled an author by the most generous interpretation of the word. Thank you also to all who read the early versions of *The Leader's Lobotomy* and shared your insights, ideas, and suggestions for making the story more interesting, engaging, and practical.

I want to also acknowledge my colleagues and friends at Hand Innovations, LLC, (HI), a company I had the privilege of leading from January 2006 to June 2008. I hope that I practiced many of the leadership principles expressed in this book, and my previous books on the subject. Your support, passion, and enthusiasm were a daily dose of adrenalin. A very special thanks to Mireya Arrieta, Dr. Joe Suarez, Javier Castaneda, Vicki Diez and Frank Kelly, who, as members of my direct staff at HI, supported me and allowed me to grow as a leader.

To Nanette Benson and Richard Johnson, who worked with me during the integration of HI to DePuy Orthopaedics after DePuy acquired HI in January 2006, thank you. Your coaching and business counsel was always on target, and kept me grounded even in the most challenging situations.

To my colleagues and friends at the Hispanic Organization for Leadership & Achievement (HOLA), thank you! Thank you for the opportunity to serve and lead as the board chairperson for this wonderful organization of talented professionals at Johnson & Johnson. I am especially grateful to Larry Montes and Kiko Morillo who served with me on the HOLA board. We helped create something good!

Finally, to Ather Williams, Curt Selquist, Russ Deyo, and Anthony Carter – four leaders of impeccable character and integrity from whom I've learned the meaning of mentorship – thank you for your guidance and friendship.

FOREWORD

When someone asks you to write the foreword for their book, you have to consider a few things. First, is this a book that can make a difference? Second, does the author have credibility in the subject area? Third, is it easy to read? Fourth, can I apply what is in the book to my life and leadership style?

After answering a resounding "YES!" to all of the above, I agreed to support this gem of a leadership book.

First, I have known Tony López for several years now. His writing and work in leadership are both inspiring and practical. In *The Leader's Lobotomy* he reminds us of the fundamentals that great leaders practice every day, and that are so easy to forget! As we climb the corporate ladder it is easy to push to the side the fundamentals such as recognizing employees properly, creating and communicating clear direction and vision, and consistently managing and driving people development and succession planning. Leaders often forget that they must create an organizational culture in which diversity is not only honored, but also leveraged as a competitive advantage. They sometimes forget that they must ensure that leaders throughout the organization, at all levels, do in fact lead! These are the ways this book can make a difference in your leadership style and leadership life.

Second, I have watched as Tony has not only written about this subject, but has put these principles into practice. From his leadership role in ETHICON, a Johnson & Johnson Company's project "REDHAND" (read his second leadership book, *Breakthrough Thinking*, to know more about this incredible project), to leading the integration, reorganization, and growth of a healthcare company in Florida, he not only believes these principles, but also lives them. I have been one of the lucky leaders to benefit from his expertise. He has all the credibility in the world!

Third, this book is not only easy to read, it is engaging and to the point. In the hectic pace of business today, none of us have the time to read *War and Peace*. *The Leader's Lobotomy* will engage you and make you laugh, and more important than anything, it will make you think. If you read it right it will also make you ACT! It is a delight.

Fourth, if you follow and practice the advice in this book, you will become a better leader - a Legacy Leader with a legacy of productivity and trust, and an example for future leaders. You will see yourself, good and bad, in this story. The challenge is to avoid the leader's lobotomy and break out to become the leaders we need to become. It isn't easy to break out of old habits. It takes practice and some risk, but as you will read, the results are worth it.

If you really aspire to be a great leader, this book will help you get there. It won't just make you a better leader; it will make you a better person.

I am honored to write the foreword for this important book. I am even more honored to call Anthony "Tony" López my friend. I have learned from him that to lead is a privilege and that to leave a legacy that we can be proud of is the ultimate goal of great leaders.

May you truly become a Legacy Leader!

Chester Elton

Chester Elton is the co-author of the runaway Wall Street Journal and BusinessWeek bestseller *A Carrot A Day*. He has been the subject of features in the New York Times and Wall Street Journal, and has been called "the apostle of appreciation" by Canada's Globe and Mail. He is also co-author of *The 24-Carrot Manager*, called "a must-read for modern-day managers" by CNN's Larry King, and the bestselling *Managing With Carrots*. Chester is vice president of performance recognition with the O.C. Tanner Recognition Company, the world's leading employee recognition firm.

INTRODUCTION

Why is it that as rookie managers grow up to be corporate leaders, they seem to forget the most basic lessons they learned along the way? Why is it that with each promotion, and with each step they take while climbing the proverbial corporate ladder, they lose basic perspective on what was important to them when they were lower on the totem pole? After all, with the possible exception of King Tut – who became King of Egypt before he was ten years old - most people who take on leadership positions have had some seasoning time in junior positions prior to becoming senior leaders.

Presumably (and thankfully, in many cases) along the way most leaders learned some good lessons about how to lead. Sadly for some, the last step in the process of climbing to the top is undergoing the leader's lobotomy – a surgery that leaves no visible scars but clearly impacts the leader's reasoning, memory, and most significantly, their effectiveness. Ultimately, as with all actions that leaders take along the way, this will affect their legacy. It will determine not only how they will be remembered, but also the long lasting impact that their leadership will have on their organization.

As with most things, repetition is the key to learning. The more we practice the more proficient we become. That is equally true whether we are learning something correctly or incorrectly. Play the wrong notes of a tune on the piano long enough, and surely you will play the song incorrectly each time. Therefore, it is not only important that we practice what we want to be good at, but that we practice it *correctly*. The same is true with leadership. It's a learned behavior. It's a practiced skill. It can be improved and perfected, but it can also be forgotten. Its effectiveness is diminished if we neglect the basics. Whether you believe that a leader is "born" or a leader is "made," there is little debate that even a leader's best skills will erode if not practiced, or worst yet, become misguided by a faulty set of priorities.

This fictional short story is my attempt at using humor to address a subject of profound significance: the leader's need to continually practice the most fundamental elements of leadership. Any similarity between characters in this short story and individuals that you may know – including yourself – is not a coincidence, and is very much done on purpose. Although it is fiction, many readers will relate to this story – which I admit takes on an autobiographical feel at times as I have committed many of the *faux pas* addressed here. Over the years I have been an admiring follower of great leaders who have never forgotten the basics of leadership. They've never lost sight of their purpose as leaders: to leave something behind of lasting worth. Regrettably, I have also been the frustrated follower of leaders who have undergone their lobotomy with irreversible consequences.

This is the third book in the *Legacy Leader* series. The first – *The Legacy Leader: Leadership With A Purpose* – began with my thesis that of all the traits a leader can and must posses, only two are non-negotiable. Those two non-negotiable qualities of a leader are *character* and *integrity*. All other qualities and skills necessary for effective leadership can be acquired via education, experience, and especially The School of Hard Knocks. Character and integrity however, are woven into the very fabric of our DNA make-up and are non-negotiable. Once character and integrity are compromised, it results in a leader's failure in reaching the maximum level of effectiveness had their character and integrity been kept whole. *The Legacy Leader* also addressed what can be labeled as the mechanics of leadership. It presented the most fundamental qualities and behaviors that leaders can, and must exhibit if they are to build "Achieving Organizations" with a personal legacy of which they can be proud.

The second book in *The Legacy Leader Series* is Breakthrough Thinking: The Legacy Leader's Role In Driving Innovation. It addressed what the Legacy Leader must do to drive teams and organizations to accomplish things they would have initially thought impossible.

In this third volume – *The Leader's Lobotomy* – we will discover what happens to leaders who, having reached positions of significant responsibility in their organizations, suddenly and without warning develop a horrible disease called PIA – Promotion-Induced Amnesia. Fortunately, there is an effective antidote to PIA. For leaders who are self aware, and who possess healthy levels of emotional intelligence, PIA is rarely fatal. However, not all are so lucky and PIA has sadly become the leading cause of premature termination of many leaders. It will no doubt claim countless other victims in the future.

As with any condition, the best cure is prevention. Even if you have not been afflicted with this debilitating illness – and it can happen to you, too – there is a cure. The best way to prevent, or cure it, is to take the antidote spelled out in this book in healthy daily doses, just like the daily glass of the vitamin-rich orange juice you drink each morning to strengthen your immune system.

Again, any resemblance to someone you know - maybe even yourself - is no accident. So beware of this epidemic disease that is spreading quickly across organizations worldwide. Vaccinate yourself with knowledge, and protect your precious Leadership Legacy with all due diligence.

CHAPTER 1

A Vision?

Jim was feeling very good about himself. He had an extra spring in his step as he made his way to his car in the parking lot of ITA, Inc. Jim had been an ITA employee for more than fifteen years, working his way up from third shift production supervisor to his most recent position as Director for U.S. Operations. He waved to a few co-workers as they entered the building to begin work on the second shift. He realized that it had been a while since he had been on the shop floor to visit the production folks on the second and third shifts. He made a mental note to do that later in the week.

He had made that mental note before.

"Hey Jim, hold up!" called Maryann as she rushed to catch up with him. Maryann was Worldwide Director of Quality Control.

"Hi, Maryann. How are you?"

"Just fine, thanks. But not as good as you," she replied with a sincere smile. "I just want to say congratulations!"

Jim shook Maryann's outstretched hand. "Thanks Maryann. I didn't think the announcement had been made yet."

"Oh it hasn't," she winked. "But, you know, I've got a few connections around here."

Jim knew that was an understatement. Maryann was more well-connected than a light bulb. She knew everything happening at ITA before anybody else.

"You are going to be a fantastic Vice President for World Wide Operations," she said.

Jim liked the way that sounded. He could not hide his pride. "Thank you, Maryann. I am really excited about this."

"You earned it," she said.

"Well, you helped me get there, that's for sure." Jim meant what he said. Maryann had been with the company for more than twenty five years, and on Jim's first day at ITA she took him under her wing and had mentored him ever since. She had been a wise and caring advisor to him over the years.

A smart, charismatic, and attractive middle-aged woman, Maryann was respected by all, admired by most, and disliked by only a few. But one thing was certain – she knew her stuff, and she breathed and lived ITA's business. In Jim's mind, she was a strong and driven leader. Maryann had never made it to the executive ranks, but it wasn't for lack of skill or ability. It was a matter of personal choice. She never wanted it.

"Now the hard work begins, Jim," Maryann warned. "Whatever you do, promise me you will not forget the lessons you've learned along the way."

Jim looked puzzled.

"Maryann!" called a voice from the second floor window. "You have an urgent call from the Lyon office."

"Ahhrr," she said with mock frustration. "The French! Will they never leave me alone? Got to run; see you in the morning, Mr. VP."

"Okay. See you in the morning."

Jim started to walk toward the parking lot again, but suddenly turned back and shouted out to Maryann just as she was about to enter the building.

"Hey, Maryann! What lessons are you talking about?"

"All of them!" she replied without missing a step. She disappeared into the building.

Jim stood frozen for a moment. *What did Maryann mean by that?*

"Hey Jim," Perry said as he zoomed by on his bicycle.

Jim snapped back to reality. "Oh, hey Perry," he said absently. He continued his walk toward the car. It was parked in the south lot, affectionately known as the "Loser's Lot." Jim smiled at the realization that this was one of the last times he would have to park back there. The VP title carried with it a larger office with a view of the small, picturesque lake on ITA's property, a much larger salary, a staff of eight directors, and a coveted parking spot close to the building's main entrance.

He finally made it to his car before he realized just how hot it was that day. Jim opened the car door, and a rush of superheated air from inside his Acura TL hit his face. He winced.

———————

"Hello?" Jim said into his cell phone.

"Are you on your way home?"

Jim recognized the sweet voice of his bride of ten years, Marisol. "Yes, I just left the office, and I'll be home in about thirty minutes or so."

"I made reservations at Torrence. They are chilling the champagne," Marisol said with a hint of flirting in her voice. "And I am wearing something spectacular."

Jim grinned. "I am sure you will look incredible." That was nothing if not the truth. Marisol was a beautiful and sophisticated woman. A labor law attorney by day and a cycling fanatic by night, she enjoyed her long quiet rides in the evening, when the sun was not too hot and the days lasted until almost nine thirty. "I guess I have to dress up also?"

"Of course," Marisol demanded. "I already picked out a suit for you."

"I have to wear a suit?" Jim hated wearing suits.

"Yes, a suit. We are going to a show after dinner, and Keith and Tina will be joining us for the show."

"Keith and Tina are coming with us?" Jim asked. Keith Lawrence had been the president of ITA for about three years, and he and Jim had become good friends. Marisol and Tina were as close as sisters.

"Surprise!" she said, proud of herself for keeping the secret for over a week. She knew about his promotion before he did! "Now, hurry home."

As he hung up the phone, in his mind he could smell the sweet perfume that his wife usually wore. He was so proud of that woman! The daughter of immigrant parents, Marisol had arrived in the United States at age thirteen, unable to speak more than a few words in English.

She had a work ethic and a passion for life like no one else Jim had ever met. Fiercely competitive, self-driven and motivated, she ultimately rose to the top of her high school class, graduating number one and earning academic scholarships to every school she applied to.

Most amazing to Jim was how she had mastered English. She was now fluent in both her native Spanish and English, which she spoke with out a hint of an accent. Along the way she had also learned Italian and a bit of French. Now, she worked tirelessly to promote labor laws to improve corporate efficiencies while protecting the rights of all employees. Jim genuinely admired his wife.

————

Traffic was unusually heavy for this early in the afternoon. The two-lane highway that took Jim home each day passed a few small towns, and there always seemed to be a bit of a slow down as drivers watched out for local cops.

Jim's mind was not on his driving. He was deep in thought about his new position. He had worked so hard toward this. He was bypassed for the position a few years earlier and almost made the mistake of leaving the company then. Maryann had talked him into staying. Somehow she had managed to tell Jim that he was not ready for the position without making him feel bad about it. Now as he looked back, he realized that she had been right. He had needed a few more years to grow as a leader before tackling the enormous challenge now ahead of him.

"Bet you think your poop don't stink now, huh?"

The deep voice with a strong New York City accent almost scared Jim out of his seat belt. He yelled as he looked to his right to find a strange man sitting in the passenger seat.

"Who the heck are you? And how did you get in my car?" Jim asked startled, his eyes wide open.

"I'm Ted," the man said as he stuck a huge cigar in his mouth and puffed on it. It was lit, but there was no smoke. "I just sorta appeared, you know what I mean?"

"No, I don't know what you mean," Jim replied, half scared and half angry. "You better get out of my car right now or you are going to be in big trouble." Jim had no idea what trouble he was referring to, but he was trying to hide his fear by sounding tough.

The driver in the car behind Jim's leaned on his horn impatiently at Jim's inaction after the red light had been green for more than five seconds.

"Green means go," the cigar smoking man said.

"I am not moving this car until you get out. I mean it, get out!"

"Relax, Jim Givens of 13244 Westward Drive. You are thirty-nine years of age, married ten years to the former Marisol Butero, thirty-five – and a gorgeous woman by the way – you have no children, you have a Labrador retriever, you have a bachelor's degree in mechanical engineering, an MBA from Duke, played high school and college baseball. You like to fish and play soccer. You prefer red wine, although Marisol is a white wine type, which makes it tough at restaurants sometimes." The man was rattling off the details in a rapid monotone, as if he were playing them back from a recorder. "Shall I continue?"

"Look mister, I don't know who you are or how you know so much about me, but I'm calling the police." Jim reached for his cell phone and dialed 9-1-1.

"Your phone has no signal," Ted said confidently.

Jim looked at the screen on his phone. He saw four bars, indicating a strong signal. "Guess you don't know everything after all," he said as he brought the phone back to his ear.

"Look again," Ted ordered.

His phone was dead.

"Okay, what do you want?"

By now there were a dozen cars behind him, beeping their horns in frustration. "You can start by getting out of the way before you become a victim of road rage."

Jim, unsure of what else to do, stepped gently on the gas and began moving forward. "So, are you going to tell me who you are?"

"I told you, my name is Ted. I am your CGA," Ted replied sarcastically.

"CGA? What's that?"

"Corporate Guardian Angel," Ted said with disgust. He shook his head. "Boy, is that stupid. That is such a dumb title. You think they could come up with a better acronym."

"You are my Corporate Guardian Angel? Is this a new program instituted by ITA?" Jim asked, trying to make sense of this strange man who appeared out of thin air and was now sitting in his car.

"Nope, it's nothing like that. Just a silly program started about five years ago when someone upstairs decided that too many leaders were acting as if they had gotten lobotomies and were suffering from PIA," Ted said sounding serious.

"PIA?" Jim asked. He was starting to wonder if he was the subject of some master practical joke.

"Promotion-Induced Amnesia."

"Promotion-Induced Amnesia?" Jim smiled, now convinced that he was the butt of a joke. "Okay man, who put you up to this? It was Derek, wasn't it? Jose?"

"Hey listen, if you think this is a practical joke then the joke is on me. I am stuck with you for as long as it takes to prevent you from getting PIA."

Jim sped into the right lane and made a sharp turn into the empty parking lot of a small restaurant off the highway. He brought the car to a screeching halt, shut the car off, took the keys out of the ignition and bolted from the car.

Ted rolled his eyes. "Why me?" he said, looking up and shaking his head. "Why do I always get the goofy ones? You always give me the assignments that no one else wants."

There was no audible response, but a moment later Ted sighed and said, "Fine, fine, I'll do it." He stepped out of the car and shouted to Jim.

"Get back in the car, dufus."

Jim was pacing like a caged animal. Then he started pointing at Ted and shouting for him to leave his car.

Ted rolled his eyes incredulously and hollered, "No one else can see me but you, so right now everyone passing by thinks you are yelling at your car."

"Hey mister, are you okay?" a young man asked as he drove by slowly.

"I'm trying to get that man to leave me alone!" Jim said before he realized how silly and desperate he sounded.

"What man, mister?"

"I'm talking about that man in my car!" Jim said pointing to his car.

The young man looked at the car and saw only the car. "Sir, there is no one in your car." He rolled up his window and drove away, shaking his head.

"I told you,'" Ted said, shrugging his shoulders. "I'm an *angel*, brainiac. I choose who I will allow to see me. Today, you're the lucky one. So hurry up and get in the car. The sooner we get this done, the sooner I can be out of your hair."

Ted leaned back in his seat and puffed on his cigar.

Jim approached the car and looked inside the window. He studied Ted for the first time. He appeared to be in his fifties. He was balding, and the hair he had left was salt and pepper colored with a beard to match. He wore deck shoes with no socks, a pair of khaki pants, and a golf polo shirt. He had a bit of a beer gut but was in fair shape for a man – or angel – of his age. Jim furled his brow and stared hard at the man. Ted reminded him of a cross between Alan King, Don Rickles and George Burns.

"Anyone ever tell you that you look like Alan King?" Jim asked.

"I get that a lot."

"So, you're an angel?"

"Not quite! Working on it though," Ted said, looking straight ahead.

"So, you are a cigar-smoking angel?"

"It's hell! I've been puffing on the same cigar for twenty years and I get nothing: no smoke, no flavor, just air."

"Why don't you quit?" Jim asked sarcastically.

"I don't quit, kid. Quitting is for losers!"

"Okay, so what are you supposed to do for me?" Jim asked.

"Simple. Help you avoid getting a leader's lobotomy and keep you from falling prey to PIA as so many other leaders do, day in and day out."

"What's in it for you?" The businessman in Jim was coming out.

"I get my wings," Ted said sarcastically.

"Oh, my goodness! Really?" Jim asked with childlike wonder.

"No, not really," Ted grunted. "What do you think this is, 'It's A Wonderful Life?' You are not Jimmy Stewart, I am not Clarence, and we are definitely not in Bedford Falls. Just get in the car."

Jim stepped back from the car. "This is not happening," he said, shutting his eyes tightly. "This is not happening."

"Okay, I don't have time for this. I'm leaving," Ted said. The car's engine magically roared on and the car began moving forward.

Jim looked down at the car keys still in his hand, and sprinted after the car. "No wait, wait! Ted! I believe you."

"Okay then, let's go. You're going to be late for dinner."

Jim settled uneasily into the driver's seat, took a deep breath and pulled back onto the highway. He looked straight ahead and did not even blink.

"Look," Ted said, finally breaking the silence. "I know this is a bit strange for you."

"Strange?" Jim shot back nervously. "Why would this be strange? I mean just because a ghost…"

"Angel," Ted said.

"Sorry," Jim continued. "I mean, yeah, it's really common for an angel to simply appear in my car. It happens every day."

"No need to get snippy, Jimmy," Ted smiled. "Is it okay if I call you Jimmy?"

Jim looked at him with contempt.

"Okay, note to self; don't call him Jimmy," Ted said, as an elegant little leather bound notebook and quill pen magically appeared, floating in thin air in front of Ted's face. The pen glided across the page under its own power and scribed the words Ted had just spoken; then both the pen and the notebook disappeared.

"I'll leave you now for a while," Ted said. "I just wanted to drop in, introduce myself and get you over the initial shock."

"Don't rush back," Jim said under his breath, relieved that his hallucination was coming to an end.

"What's that, Jimmy?"

"I said, 'how about that.'" He looked to his right and found the passenger seat empty. Ted had vanished.

––––––––

By the time Jim and Marisol returned home after the show, Jim had forgotten all about Ted. He smiled to himself as he lay down next to his wife. She was already half asleep.

"Thanks for a great night, dear," he said softly into her ear.

"You're welcome, Mr. Vice President," she said in a whisper as she slipped into a cozy sleep.

Jim went to bed confident that all was well, and that tomorrow was going to be a great day.

––––––––

"Wake up, sleeping beauty," Ted said in a raspy voice.

Jim woke up, startled. "You? I thought you were…"

"Gone?" Ted said. "No, but you will wish I was gone soon. Now get up, we've got work to do."

Jim looked at the alarm clock. "It's 4:30 in the morning, and please keep your voice down or you'll wake my wife."

"She can't hear me, genius. Remember – angel, kinda-like-a-ghost? Now get down to your office. It's time for lesson number one on what you should not forget as a leader."

For the first time, Jim was intrigued by what Ted had to say. If this was a figment of his imagination, he might as well go with it.

By the time Jim got downstairs to his home office, Ted was already sitting on the desk.

He pointed at the desk chair. "Sit," he ordered. Jim complied.

"Now pay attention, buttercup. Much of what I am going to tell you will seem simple and even trivial. But mark my words; these simple truths are often overlooked by the most seasoned leaders, and even by some good ones."

Jim leaned forward in the chair and stared intently at Ted. "Now, the notebook in front of you," Ted continued.

Jim looked down. There was nothing in front of him. "I don't see a notebook."

"That's because it's invisible," Ted explained. "You will only see it when I give you something to write in it, or when you need to be reminded of something I told you to write down. Got it?"

"Got it," Jim repeated, only half confident that he indeed had it.

"Okay, leaders who suffer from PIA exhibit many symptoms, most of which are visible to everyone around them except for themselves. My job is to teach you about the rules you must never forget as a leader. If you keep these rules in mind at all times, you will avoid the leader's lobotomy and you will not die from PIA. Think of these lessons as antidotes to a terrible poison. Follow me so far?"

"I think so."

"Good. Now take your invisible pen."

There was now a fancy leather-bound notebook and a beautiful gold and white feathered pen on the desk in front of him. Jim reached for the pen and as he picked it up, he noticed a glow coming from it. He smiled.

"It's pretty cool, right?" Ted said.

"Yeah. Cool."

"Okay Jimbo, what's the very first thing you must never forget as a leader?"

Jim squinted as he searched his mind for an answer. He had read all the best books on the subject. This was his chance to really impress Ted.

"Always do the right thing," Jim announced proudly. Ted stared at him, expressionless. Jim realized that this was not the answer Ted was looking for.

"Set organizational priorities?" Ted just stared at Jim.

"Direct, align, and motivate people?" Jim said, now grasping for an answer that would get Ted to stop staring at him.

"I told you that these rules were going to be simple, trivial, and in some cases painfully obvious. Try again. What was the first thing you wanted to know from any new leader you ever worked for?"

"I wanted to know where he wanted to take the organization!" Jim answered. "What his vision was for the organization."

"Bingo! He can be taught after all!" Ted mocked Jim playfully, dancing around to the other side of the desk. Both Ted and Jim laughed.

"Write this down: *A leader must never forget that having a clear vision is of paramount importance!*"

Jim wrote on the magic notebook with the magic pen, and gold ink captured the thought on the very first page of the notebook.

"How many times did you and your buddies at work sit in the cafeteria and complain that your boss had no clear vision? Even you guys were confused about where you all were driving the organization. Remember?"

Jim nodded in affirmation. It was true. Many times he and his colleagues spoke of that very issue.

"Don't ever forget that, as a leader, having a clear vision is an absolute must. Got that?"

"I got it!" Jim said confidently.

Jim stared at Ted waiting for him to continue.

"What are you waiting for then, sleeping beauty? Get to work. What's your vision? Think about it. Write it down. I'm going back to bed."

With that, Ted disappeared, and Jim was left alone with only the glow of his magic pen to illuminate the darkness around him.

"What's my vision?" Jim asked himself. He settled back in his chair to think about it.

Antidote to
Promotion-Induced Amnesia (PIA)

Dose #1
**"Leaders must never forget that having a
clear vision is of paramount importance."**

CHAPTER 2

Communicate or Fail

Jim got in his car and made his way to the office early. He had a confidence about him – more so than usual, because he was armed with his well thought out vision. He knew where he wanted to take his new organization. Jim had always imagined what he would do if he was in charge, but this was the first time he had actually organized his thoughts into a clear and concise statement.

Jim parked his car closer to the front entrance than he normally did, which was one of the perks of arriving earlier. He would soon be assigned reserved parking spot number fourteen, but he did not feel comfortable parking there today. He was not sure if news of his promotion had been made public yet, and besides, the guy who had parking space number fourteen assigned to him was still packing boxes in his old office. He was quietly being fired and Jim did not want to add to his misery.

"Good morning, BJ," Jim said, waving at the golden haired woman at the front desk in the lobby. She had been with ITA since the company's first day, thirty-three years before.

"Good morning, Jim," she answered, with the same pleasant smile she always wore. "Hey, congratulations," she said, lowering her voice even though no one else was in the lobby.

"Thanks BJ."

"You are going to be great," she assured him.

Jim smiled and swiped his access card across the electronic lock to gain access to the building's main corridor. Instinctively, he turned left, then right, then left again to reach his office. Two workers had beaten him there and were already packing to move him to his new office, upstairs on executive row.

_____

By noon, Jim was completely moved into his new third floor office. He sat behind his desk, not sure of what to do next. A beep from his computer saved him from thinking.

"What are you waiting for?" the Instant Message read. Jim was puzzled.

"Well?" the second message asked.

Jim leaned into the computer keyboard and wrote, "I don't follow your message?"

"Have you always been this slow?" Ted's raspy voice filled the office.

Jim nearly jumped out of his seat.

"You are going to have to stop popping in like that!" Jim complained.

"I'm an angel. Popping in is what we do," he said with a fiendish grin. "So, what are you doing?"

"I'm working."

"Working? What are you working on?"

"Stuff, that's what," Jim said defensively.

"Important stuff?" Ted pushed. "Did you finish your vision statement?"

"I did," Jim announced proudly. He pulled out a sheet of paper from his computer bag and handed it to Ted. It had a short, concise statement that Jim had written before sunrise that morning, after having tossed several earlier attempts into the recycling bin.

Ted nodded with approval. "It's good," he pronounced. "Not bad, kid. But there's something missing."

"Missing?"

"Yeah, you're definitely missing something here."

Jim was sure he wasn't. He felt very good about the vision he had drafted. It spelled out exactly where he wanted to go with the organization.

"Who wrote this?" Ted asked, trying to hint at the answer to his question.

"Well, I did," Jim said. Then he shook his head and smiled. "Ah, yes, I know – my team's input! *That's* what's missing."

"Give that man a cigar!" Ted said, as a cigar immediately materialized in his right hand. "Darn! No smoke."

"Write this down," Ted ordered. The magic notebook and pen appeared on Jim's desk. Jim eagerly picked up the pen.

"Leaders must never forget to give their followers a say in developing the vision," Ted dictated. "Got it? Good. You see, a mistake that many leaders make is not involving their followers in developing the vision. That's not to say that you as the leader can't guide where they land with the vision statement. You can! In fact, you must. But involving the team in the process of writing it will help crystallize it in all of your minds. And you'll gain their buy-in and ownership of the vision at the same time."

Jim looked at Ted with admiration – and surprise. He never ceased to be amazed that this gruff, grumpy old man was so profound in his thinking.

"I know, I know," Ted smirked. "I impress myself sometimes, too." He and Jim chuckled.

"In other words," Jim said, "I have to know where I want to go, but I have to get my team to help develop and write the vision statement if I want us to succeed – and have staying power."

"That's the ticket. You see, the actual words are not that important. What is important is that they understand where you want to go, that they buy into it, and that they can verbalize it so they actually own it along with you."

"Ok, I got it," Jim said.

"So write it down then!" Ted ordered. "Leaders must never forget to give their followers a say in developing the vision."

Antidote to Promotion-Induced Amnesia (PIA)

Dose #2
"Leaders must never forget to give their followers a say in developing the vision."

"So, let's get back to my original question. What are you waiting for?"

Ted got a blank stare from Jim.

"Okay," Ted continued, "this will work better if you bring your brain with you when we talk. What do you think you need to do next?"

"If you're thinking that I need to get the team together and lay down ground rules, I think maybe it would be best to wait a bit and let people get used to the new change first," Jim proclaimed with confidence.

Just then Samantha Higgins knocked on Jim's door and peeked her head inside.

"Hi Jim."

"Um, hi Sam. What's up?" Jim asked nervously, momentarily forgetting that only he could see or hear Ted.

"A few of your new staff are asking to see you today," she said. "I guess they all want some direction from you. Should I schedule time with each of them?"

Jim looked at Ted, who raised his eyebrows, sat back on the sofa and puffed smugly on his cigar. "Humph! Imagine that!" Ted said.

"Yeah, yeah, I got it," Jim howled in Ted's direction.

"Sorry?" Samantha asked.

"Sorry Sam, just thinking out loud. Let's get the team together at three o'clock this afternoon."

"Okay. Will do," Sam said with a smile, and closed the door behind her.

Even before Samantha had closed the door Ted began speaking. "The best way for you to avoid PIA will be to remind yourself often of how you thought and felt when you were the follower. Think about *what* you wish your boss had done differently, *how* you wish he had done it, and *when* you wish he had done it. Think about the many cafeteria conversations with your colleagues, and the things you all complained about when talking about the leaders in your organization. Remember how you wished the boss would have thought about this or that. It's a perspective you must never lose as a leader. It's gold!"

Jim nodded. "Common sense," he said.

"Exactly! One of the main ingredients in the recipe for a good leader," Ted said. "Common sense!"

"What are the other ingredients?"

"Aha!" Ted exclaimed, "I see I have your interest now."

Jim was indeed hooked.

"One step at a time," Ted continued. "Let me get this one out of the way first, because it's so painfully obvious and it frustrates me that so many leaders totally blow it. Write this down: *Leaders must never forget that communication is their number one job.*"

Jim looked up from the notebook.

"Come on now, give me a break!" Jim complained. "I mean, that just goes without saying. We all communicate. We send e-mails, voice mails, faxes, and letters. We go to meetings, stop people in the halls and catch up, we have brainstorm sessions. All we ever do is communicate. In fact, sometimes I think we waste too much time with all the e-mails and voice mails. Sometimes I wish leaders would not talk so much."

"Oh, you certainly do send plenty of e-mails, voice mails, faxes, and letters!" Ted replied. "And boy, do you people love to have meetings and brainstorming sessions – although they are usually more like brain*farting* sessions. I could not agree with you more that leaders should shut up more often. But let's get to the video tape and see what you and your buddies have to say about communications."

With that, an image appeared in front of Jim like a three dimensional hologram. He recognized the scene. He was sitting at a table in ITA's cafeteria with four other director-level members of the operations staff.

"You remember this?"

"I do," Jim said.

"Do you remember what you guys were talking about?"

"Yeah, we were complaining about how poor communications were in the organization, and how different VP's were pulling us in different directions."

"But that wasn't all, was it?"

Jim knew what was coming.

"You guys also played a little game, didn't you? Let's watch."

The frozen video image came to life, and for a moment Jim felt like he was having an out-of-body experience. He heard himself suggest that the five of them conduct a simple experiment:

> *"Lets each write down what the organizational vision is for ITA. Also write down what you think are the top three priorities our Operations Organization is supposed to be focusing on."*

Jim watched the video as the four men and one woman each put their heads down and scribbled their thoughts on napkins.

Ted let him watch for a bit longer, then broke the silence with, "Do you need to see more?"

Jim remembered with crystal clarity what had happened.

"No, there's no need to see any more."

"What was the outcome?" Ted asked smugly.

Jim sighed. "We each had a different version of the vision, and between us we had twelve uniquely different things we thought the organization should be focusing on."

"And you guys were the mangers! Can you imagine what would happen if your employees had done the same little exercise? Jimmy boy, when it comes to communications, the leader can't do enough of it!"

Jim nodded in agreement.

"It's not about *quantity*; it's all about the *quality* of the communication," Ted explained. "Leaders should always strive to improve their effectiveness as communicators, and to do so, they must keep a few simple rules in mind: First, communicate to inform, not to impress. Two, communicate to clarify, not to confuse; and three, communicate directly, not with double talk."

"As simple as ABC, right?" Jim asked.

"Amazing that so many leaders screw it up, huh?"

"Yes it is."

"Are you going to write it down?"

The notebook and pen magically reappeared, and Jim made the entry.

"Any questions?" Ted asked. "If not, school's out for today."

"I guess I have a meeting to prepare for now," Jim said to himself.

Ted disappeared, but his voice thundered these last three powerful words: "Communicate or Fail!"

Antidote to
Promotion-Induced Amnesia (PIA)

Dose #3
"Leaders must not forget that communications is their number one job"

Communicate to inform, not to impress
Communicate to clarify, not to confuse
Communicate directly, not with double talk

CHAPTER 3

Listening. What's that again?

Several weeks later

J im was frustrated as he read the meeting minutes.

"Hey Jim, got a second?" Brad asked, having just appeared in Jim's office doorway. Brad was the director who replaced Jim when he was promoted almost a month earlier.

"Hi Brad. What's up?"

Brad sat in the chair in front of Jim's desk and began talking. Jim tried to listen, but his mind kept wandering back to the e-mail he had just been reading.

As Brad continued to explain his dilemma, the phone rang.

Jim looked over and saw the caller ID. It was Keith, the president of ITA. "Better get this," Jim said, interrupting Brad and reaching for the phone. "It's the boss."

"Sure," Brad said, not really meaning it.

Jim spoke with Keith for about three minutes. The first thirty seconds they spoke about business. The other two and a half were spent recounting the previous weekend's golf outing.

"Sorry, Brad. Please go ahead," Jim said as he hung up the phone. He really had no idea where Brad had left off.

Brad jumped right back where he left off without missing a beat. A few seconds after Brad resumed speaking, there was a knock on the door.

"Sorry to interrupt," Cliff Morris said, not really meaning it. "Jim, we need to finalize the headcount numbers today."

Cliff was ITA's CFO, and he was all business.

"I know Cliff," Jim said. "I'll come see you after lunch, okay?"

Cliff turned and left as quickly as he arrived.

Jim shook his head and sighed. "Sorry."

Brad shrugged his shoulders and continued his monologue. After a few minutes, Jim gave Brad some suggestions and a couple of follow ups. Brad thanked him and left.

––––––––––

Jim was back reading his e-mail again and found himself becoming frustrated as he read one lengthy message.

"So, you got it all figured out?" Ted's burly voice boomed from the corner of Jim's office, where he had magically appeared.

Startled, Jim asked, "Where in the world have you been?" He sounded like a worried father.

"Did you miss me, dear?" Ted teased.

"You pop in a few times and then you disappear for three and a half weeks. What's that about?"

"Hey, you are not the only leader on my route, you know. Unfortunately there are more leaders with PIA than you can shake a stick at," Ted said.

"So, what do you want now?" Jim asked, dismissing Ted's explanation.

"Why are you so frustrated, Jimmy?"

"I'm sorry," Jim said. "Didn't mean to be so short. It's this darn message. It's the minutes from the staff meeting we had a few days ago."

"And?" Ted prodded.

"On at least three occasions it says, 'Jim wants this,' or 'Jim wants that,'" Jim complained. "I was only making suggestions, trying to generate discussion. I wasn't trying to impose my will!"

Ted smiled. "School's in session. Write this down." The magic gold and white feather pen and leather bound notebook suddenly materialized from thin air.

Ted continued, *"Leaders must never forget that their words can be mistaken and taken as gospel by their followers."*

As he finished writing, Jim looked up, still frustrated. "So what am I supposed to do, say nothing at meetings? Not make any suggestions or give any direction?"

"The answers are no, no, and definitely no," Ted said. "You must say something. You must make suggestions, and you surely must give direction. The key is how you do these things."

Jim put down the pen and looked intently at Ted.

"Before you speak, listen. Before you make suggestions, seek the opinions of others. Whenever possible, if the direction suggested by someone else is one you can agree with or line up with, then go with it. Giving one of the members the credit for the team's direction is incredibly powerful. You will motivate that person to come up with other great ideas, and you will be encouraging others to contribute as well. But like I said, you have to listen, first and foremost."

"Well, listening is not my problem," Jim complained. "I listen well."

"Oh, really? You mean, like you listened to Brad earlier?"

Antidote to
Promotion-Induced Amnesia (PIA)

Dose #4
"Leaders must never forget that their words can be mistaken and taken as gospel by their followers."

"I listened to him before I told him what I thought he should do."

"Yeah, but did you *really* listen to him? What was his bottom line issue?" Ted pushed.

Jim thought about it for a moment. He really wasn't sure what Brad's concerns actually were.

"You interrupted him at least twice with phone calls and drop-in visitors, and you could stop yourself from continually glancing at your e-mail."

Ted was right and Jim knew it.

"Write this down," Ted continued, *"Leaders must not forget how to actively listen!"*

Antidote to
Promotion-Induced Amnesia (PIA)

Dose #5
"Leaders must not forget how to listen!"

"Last time I saw you, we covered the leader's need to be a constant communicator, but that does not mean that you are to talk all the time! The leader that talks too much is a fool. They must be able to discern when it's their time to speak, and when it's their turn to listen. Communication can be a one-way street with a pompous leader. If during a board meeting, the CEO is speaking more than ten percent of the time, he or she is talking too much."

"By that measure, they all speak too much," Jim complained.

"And yet, by and large, leaders violate this important rule constantly and spend upwards of seventy or eighty percent of the time dominating a discussion," Ted continued. "Then, they act surprised when they ask for input from their staff and all they get are blank stares, or at best a no-impact, politically correct statement from a few people trying to kiss the boss' rear."

"I know the kind you're talking about," Jim jumped in, giving Ted a chance to catch his breath.

"Everybody does. They are often called 'yes people,' but I prefer calling them what they are, which is 'butt kissers.'" As he said those words, the booming sound of thunder resonated throughout Jim's office, startling both of them.

Ted looking up at the ceiling and said, "Okay, okay, I'm sorry. I'm just calling it like I see it. I'll keep it clean." He looked at Jim, winked and whispered, "They don't like it when I use colorful language."

"Anyway, I have come to believe that listening is the most important communication skill a leader can possess. I have also come to the conclusion that listening is one of the most difficult skills for a leader to develop. Contrary to popular belief, listening is not a passive activity. It is an active sport requiring extreme concentration, focus, and a Herculean amount of effort."

Jim jumped in saying, "For leaders who are accustomed to being heard, it must be hard to be quiet and start listening instead."

"You're right. It's darn near impossible for some," Ted said. "But I will tell you this: not being able to listen is a debilitating weakness that minimizes their effectiveness as communicators, reduces their ability to influence followers, and diminishes their impact as motivators – all of which translates to a lousy leader."

Ted paused and puffed hard on his long cigar.

"Listening is an active sport, Jimbo," Ted repeated. "If you can't listen, you are missing at least half the communications. Don't just shut up and listen, pay attention! Give feedback to confirm what you hear. There are few things more important for a leader to do well than listening. People get promoted, and suddenly they think they just got a license to talk."

"Okay Ted, I hear you on this. But I've known most of the people working for me for a long time. We have been colleagues for years, in many cases. So they know my style, and I know theirs."

"Do you think that this hasn't all changed now that you're the boss?" Ted said mockingly.

"These guys are my friends."

"Stop, stop, stop!" Ted said, waving his hands in the air. "Did you like your boss? The guy you replaced?"

"Very much."

"Were you friends?" Ted continued.

"I'd say so, yes," Jim answered confidently.

"Did you always tell him the truth?"

Jim paused, startled by the candid nature of the question. Ted's steel blue eyes pierced him.

"Yes, pretty much." Jim said.

"Pretty much told the truth? Well, that's like being just a little bit pregnant." Ted smiled.

"No, no," Jim stammered. "I mean, I told him what he needed to know."

"Really? Should I play back a little something from the video archive?" The virtual holographic screen sparkled to life before Jim's face. "Shall I play some selected footage?"

"Video archive? No, that's not necessary. I get your point."

"Do you?" Ted insisted.

"Yeah, yeah, I get it. I did not tell him everything. Satisfied?"

"Why is that, Jim?"

"Because there were things I could take care of myself."

"That's good. But why else?"

"There were some things I'd rather not tell him."

"Right! And what about your colleagues? Did they tell him everything?"

"No," Jim answered.

"That's right, Beavis. So what makes you think your people are going to treat you any differently?"

Jim shrugged in defeat.

"Write this down," Ted commanded. "Pay close attention because I'm coming at you fast. *Leaders should never forget that people around them don't always feel comfortable telling them everything they need to know. What leaders hear in meetings and other settings is sometimes only partially true.*"

Jim wrote as quickly as he could.

Ted was about to continue speaking when Jim motioned for him to hold on.

"Wait – why is that, Ted? Why can't we just speak what's on our mind?" Jim asked.

Antidote to
Promotion-Induced Amnesia (PIA)

Dose #6
"Leaders should never forget that people around them don't always feel comfortable telling them everything they need to know."
And
"What leaders hear in meetings and other settings is sometimes only partially true or complete."

Antidote to
Promotion-Induced Amnesia (PIA)

Dose #7
"Leaders should remember that their followers could sometimes be intimidated by them."

"Why don't people always speak their minds? Great question. The reasons are many, but you will want to write this down. One of the reasons is that *leaders should remember that their followers can sometimes be intimidated by them.*"

"Makes sense," Jim admitted. "But what can I do about that?"

"There are a few things you can do about it. First, stay close to your people, and your people's people. Be accessible and available, and for goodness sake, get out from behind your desk and walk around the place as often as you can."

"We always did complain about our leaders seemingly being holed up in some inner sanctum somewhere, or never eating in the cafeteria with us," Jim said.

"Oh, leaders are great at coming up with excuses for not making the time to be around. They have too many meetings, too much travel, thousands of e-mails and all that nonsense. You can't imagine how much you'll learn by dropping in on someone, or sitting in the cafeteria for lunch. The informal networks of communication are the best. The more accessible you are, the more people will open up, and the less intimidating you will be to them."

"It's that simple?" Jim asked.

"It's leadership, not rocket science! Common sense rules, man!"

"That doesn't really answer why people are, as you say, intimidated by their leaders so often."

"Okay, consider this," Ted began. "Remember when Paul became vice president of marketing? He had been in marketing here at ITA for how long before that?"

"A long time," Jim recalled.

"Yeah. He came to ITA as a junior product manager, and over a fifteen-year period he worked hard and climbed through the different levels in marketing. He was very well liked, wasn't he?"

"Sure he was. He was a hell of a nice guy and everyone liked working with him."

"Yet as soon as he became a VP, what happened? How did you and the other guys at the director level suddenly see him?"

"As one of 'them.'"

"One of 'them?'" Ted pushed, leading Jim toward understanding.

"You know, one of *them* – the senior board people with all the power."

"Did he change or did the people around him change?" Ted snapped back.

Jim thought about it for a minute. "Wow, I guess we probably changed our attitudes about him more than he changed his about us."

"Absolutely! You see, people sometimes disconnect themselves from their leaders simply by holding them at arms length. The reason is they are not sure if they can still pal around with the person. Whether they can still trust them, or speak with them the same way they did before. They are intimidated by the title, the position, and the power the person now wields."

"Well, that sucks!" Jim exclaimed. "You are saying that even if we don't want to be disconnected, our followers are going to disconnect from us anyway. And if we are disconnected from them, then we are disconnected from the organization as well. So regardless, we can't win!"

"You can win if you know that this happens! The problem is that leaders don't think about it. They figure nothing has changed; that people will still treat them the same way they did when they were not the big shot executive or the boss. They don't even realize that they are becoming more and more disconnected from their organizations and teams by the minute."

Ted paused for a moment, and then continued. "But if you know this is an inevitable dynamic, you can work to overcome it by being more accessible and remaining as connected with each member of your team as you can, watching your behaviors carefully so as not to create airs, and leading not just with strength but also compassion."

Jim nodded with understanding.

"Now Jim, this does not mean that in order to be liked you have to be everyone's buddy, or a pushover. In fact, you need to get used to the idea that you will not be liked by many people. It comes with the territory."

"Okay, so break it down for me, Ted. What can I do to reduce the intimidation factor for my folks?"

"First, *be accessible and approachable*. Second, *be humble*. Not a pushover, but humble. *Be a great active listener*. By listening to people, you let them know that their opinion counts. *Be direct and honest in your communications*, but also *be compassionate*. People need to hear the truth, but they don't need a ton of bricks to fall on top of them."

Jim was writing as fast as he could.

"*Become your people's champion and sponsor*. Always remember that it is about them; not about you! You take care of their needs and they'll take care of the rest."

Jim nodded in enthusiastic agreement. "That one is really important," he said to himself.

"Act consistently and with the highest level of integrity. *Earn and keep your people's trust.*"

Antidote to
Promotion-Induced Amnesia (PIA)

Dose #8
**"To reduce the intimidation factor,
leaders should:"**
Be accessible and approachable
Be humble
Be a great listener
Be direct and honest
Be a champion and sponsor
Act consistently and with integrity
Earn and keep trust
Be decisive and strong

That can take a long time, Jim thought to himself, still writing in the magic notebook.

"Not necessarily," Ted said, having read Jim's thought. "There are two ways to get your team's trust. One way is earning it over time, and you're right — that can take a while. The second way is to ask them outright to give you their trust. Promise them that you will work to keep their trust."

Jim looked up from the notebook and asked, "Just like that? Just ask them to trust you?"

"Just like that!" Ted replied.

"But what's in it for them? I mean, why would they just give you their trust?"

"Simple," Ted smiled. "It's because of what they get from you first. You promise them *your* trust. One hundred percent trust from the get go!"

"Hold on. Trusting everybody one hundred percent can be dangerous."

"You think? What are you really risking? Some people will let you down, but I can guarantee you that ninety nine out of one hundred people will work hard to keep your trust." Ted paused. "Did you catch that last part? They will work hard to keep your trust; emphasis on the 'they'!"

"So you are saying that they will have to do the work to keep my trust, not me?"

"That's right Einstein, but you will work just as hard to keep their trust. The bottom line is that it's better to have people working to maintain the trust than working over months – or even years – to earn it. It is much more effective, and saves time. And in business, time is money, right? So you can either waste time trying to have your folks earn your trust, and you working to earn theirs, or you can both start from a position of trust."

"It makes lots of sense!" Jim concluded as he resumed writing. "But what happens when someone violates your trust?"

"You deal with it quickly and directly. You may have some damage control to do, but here's the best part – your other team members will jump to your defense. They will not like the fact that 'one of them' broke the trust code, and they'll rally to your side. That's the power of trusting your people."

Ted was quiet for a moment. Finally, Jim looked up.

"What?"

"Mark these words carefully," Ted said solemnly. "*Never, ever violate the trust your followers give you. Never. Understand?*"

Jim reflected on Ted's words, letting them sink in. Finally, he nodded and said, "Understood."

"Good. Finally, *be decisive and strong*. And never shy away from taking assertive administrative action to deal with poor performance, or…"

Jim abruptly stopped writing, looked at Ted and frowned.

"What?" Ted spat out. "Am I going too fast for you?"

"No, it's just that last one. Sounds like you are saying to be tough with people who are not performing. Do you mean like firing people?"

"Absolutely! When necessary, then yes, that's exactly what you need to do."

"How's that going to help with the intimidation factor? I mean, if people get fired, doesn't that just add to the 'fear factor'?"

"You didn't let me finish my sentence. Never shy away from taking assertive administrative action to deal with poor performance, *or* from rewarding great performance often and appropriately."

Jim smiled.

"You get it, don't you? Bottom line is if someone needs to go because they are not contributing to the team or they are not performing, everybody knows it and everyone is talking about it anyway! They are wishing that their leaders would do something about it. So take care of the business that needs to be taken care of. People are not intimidated by that. In fact, they see it as sound leadership. However, you must also be able to recognize and reward people for great performance. We'll get more into that later. For now, learn to balance, kiddo. It's always about balance!"

CHAPTER 4

"Politicide"

Thanksgiving weekend

Jim was sitting in his home office. It had been a great Thanksgiving Day. This was his favorite holiday of the year. His in-laws were visiting and Jim had enjoyed his mother-in-law's fabulous cooking. The turkey was perfect and the trimmings fantastic. He and Mike, his father-in-law, had spent the afternoon watching football and shooting pool in basement game room.

Later that evening, Jim and Marisol decorated their seven-foot tall Christmas tree. Jim paid little attention to the ornaments Marisol handed him to hang on the tree. Rather, like a typical engineer, he concerned himself more with the size and uniformity of the ornaments and how evenly they were distributed to make sure the tree was well-balanced. It might have been the special way that Marisol touched Jim's hand when she handed him one particular ornament, but it caused Jim to glance at her, and that's when he noticed "the look." She smiled gently. He looked in his hand and there it was – the ornament of a baby wearing a diaper. Combined with "the look," it was a clear sign that the coming year was going to be an especially blessed one for their family.

Jim and Marisol had been thinking about having a baby, and this was her way of saying she was ready. Jim gave her a big smile, and whistling a happy tune, got back to the task at hand. The baby ornament found a special place front and center, just below the angel that adorned the top of the tree.

Everyone had gone to bed, but Jim just wasn't tired. He walked into his dimly lit, well-decorated office, sat and began thinking. He decided to begin the homework assignment he had received from Ted.

He stared down at the paper where he had written Ted's question. He imagined Ted's voice as he silently read the questions to himself:

> *Politics. Office politics, to be precise. What are they really? Give some examples of how they manifest in the office. Why do they happen, and what is the impact of letting them go on unchecked?*

He pulled out a clean sheet of paper and a pen from the left desk drawer and wrote the first question: 'What are office politics?' Much to his surprise, Jim found himself unable to come up with a simple definition for this everyday fact of office life.

"It's like they say; you may not be able to define it, but you know it when you see it," Ted said from the plush leather chair in the corner. It had become his usual spot.

Jim calmly looked up from his desk. He had expected that Ted would appear. He'd gotten used to Ted just materializing out of thin air whenever he contemplated a leadership question. "Yeah. That's exactly what I was thinking."

The two sat together in silence for a few minutes. Jim tapped his pen lightly on the desk as he stared into the darkness in Ted's direction. "Perhaps another way to think of office politics is to think more in terms of office culture."

Ted smiled slightly. He liked where Jim was going with his thought process. Jim continued, "It's about how people behave both in public forums and private meetings. It's what we say and what we don't say, and even how we say it."

Silence again.

"Well don't stop there, Jimmy. You are on the right track," Ted said at last.

"It's about agendas – but personal ones rather than for the team. It's about rumors and gossip. It's about people wasting time jockeying for position rather than positioning the team for success. It's about what we say and what we actually end up doing, and how those two things are sometimes quite different. It's about protecting our behinds rather than being vulnerable. It's about trying to impress others rather than focusing on the tasks at hand. It's about caring more about ourselves than we do about others on the team."

"What does that sound like?" Ted prompted.

"Oh gosh, it can take so many forms. Like, 'can you believe what Ted did at the meeting this morning?' or 'I'm a big fan of Ted, but he simply doesn't have a clue what he is doing.'"

"I always know what's coming when I hear a sentence that starts with 'I love so and so to death, but…' You just know the person is about to throw old 'so and so' under the bus," Ted said with a chuckle. "Office politics are productivity's worst enemy. It chokes the creativity of the team."

Jim jumped in, "Office politics are like weeds in your lawn. They just pop up and they look like grass from a distance, but if you get close enough, you see them for what they really are. And if you don't do anything about the weeds, they spread and choke the good grass. Not only that, the longer you let them grow, the harder they are to kill."

"Bingo! Give that man a cigar!" Ted shouted, and magically a cigar appeared between Jim's lips. "And to get rid of the weeds, what do you use?"

Jim removed the cigar from his mouth and admired it. "Wow, a real Cuban Montecristo? Sweet…"

"Hey! Back on task, muchacho. What do you use to get rid of weeds?"

"A herbicide, of course. But one that kills the weeds and not the grass," Jim said confidently.

"Right again, grasshopper. You are turning into a fine student after all. So write this down." The magic notebook and pen crystallized before Jim and he prepared to write. *"Leaders must remember that office politics choke the organization, and they must apply 'politicide' to get rid of it."*

Jim nodded in agreement as he wrote. "*Politicide* for *herbicide.* Nice touch with the play on words."

"Just made it up. Not bad, huh?"

"So the obvious question is, what do you do to get rid of the politics once and for all?" Jim asked.

"Well, you would have to fire everyone in the company and work pretty much by yourself, because wherever two or more are gathered, there are bound to be some politics."

"I'm surprised at you, Ted. It's not like you to be negative on this kind of thing. Are you saying that there is no way to have a politics-free work zone?"

"That's what I am saying. The best you can hope to do is create an environment where office politics are minimized. You can make sure that the impact of the politics is understood and recognized by all, and make everyone in the team accountable for working toward having a positive and effective culture."

Jim thought about it for a while. "Ok, how do I do that?"

"What do we normally say about leadership?" Ted asked.

"It's not rocket science," Jim answered.

Antidote to
Promotion-Induced Amnesia (PIA)

Dose #9
"Leaders must remember that office politics choke the organization."

"Right. There is no exception to that rule. You hit the nail on the head when you compared office politics to the organizational culture. And the person that can most influence the organizational culture is…?"

"The leader."

"Correctomundo," Ted said. "The leader. You! You can and must set the tone for what the organizational culture of your team will be. That means you also set the tone for what the office politics will be like. There are four simple things that the leader can do to kill office politics. Write these down:

1. *Insist on – and model – open, honest, and transparent communication.*
2. *Make it clear that you will not tolerate those who gossip or spread rumors.*
3. *Call out behaviors inconsistent with the culture you want to create. Encourage and expect others to do the same.*
4. *Host frequent town hall meetings and address all issues that may be "wandering" around the halls.*

"Got it?" Ted asked.

"Got it. This all makes perfect sense. I can't wait to put it into practice," Jim replied.

"Terrific!" Ted exclaimed. "*Now* you can enjoy that cigar."

Antidote to
Promotion-Induced Amnesia (PIA)
Dose #10
"To get rid of office politics, leaders must use 'politicide.'"
1. Insist on – and model – transparent communication.
2. Don't tolerate those who gossip or spread rumors.
3. Call out behaviors inconsistent with the culture. Encourage and expect others to do the same.
4. Host frequent town hall meetings to deal with rumors and other issues adversely affecting the work environment.

CHAPTER 5

"Corporate Jealousy"

Dawn had just finished setting up the projector and the laptop computer in the HR conference room. She had been planning for this meeting for a few weeks now, but it wasn't something she was really looking forward to. It was the annual performance audit and succession planning session. As the HR partner to operations, this was her third year managing the process, and she knew that it was flawed from the start.

Jim was back in his office gathering a few papers and preparing for the same meeting. He actually looked forward to these sessions.

"Performance appraisal time?" Ted's voiced boomed throughout Jim's office.

"Oh, hi Ted," Jim said casually. By now he was not startled when Ted appeared from nothingness. "Yeah, we are doing performance appraisals and succession planning today. It's our talent scope process."

"So, tell me, how do you folks go about it?"

"Well, we have every director present each of their people, one at a time. They talk about the person's accomplishments for the year, the projects they were on, and how they went about obtaining their results."

"What else?"

"Then we discuss it as a team. Everyone has a chance to give their opinion about the person's performance and interactions as a team member."

"Yeah? And?"

"Well, then the director proposes a rating for the individual. If there is agreement on the rating, we move on. If not, we debate it until we reach resolution to the rating. After that, we talk about potential next assignments for the person, and some ideas for development. That's the part I like most because we are talking about how to help the person grow and progress."

"Sounds pretty good. Most companies don't even do that much," Ted said.

Jim looked at him suspiciously. "A compliment from you? That's certainly not like you. You have something to say about the process?"

"Well, let me ask you this: how's the process working out for you and the organization?"

"Pretty good, I'd say," Jim answered confidently. "I mean, I'm a product of that process."

"Hmmm."

"What do you mean, hmmm? If you have something to say, let's have it," Jim challenged.

"Nothing wrong with the process. It's just that what you see is not always what you get, that's all."

"Now you're talking in riddles? Remember that whole thing about communicate to inform, not confuse?"

"It's simple, Jimmy boy. There are three things to remember about meetings in which people's performance and development plans are discussed."

As he spoke, the familiar magic notebook and pen appeared before Jim, who instinctively grabbed both.

"One, nowhere are politics more prevalent than in these meetings. Two, people play favorites with those they like most. And three, people sometimes lie to improve their position over someone else. You know why?"

Jim thought about it, but did not answer.

"Corporate jealousy," Ted said.

Jim nodded.

"You know what I mean, don't you?" Ted asked.

"Jealousy between peers, and also between peers and their bosses, right?"

"Oh yeah, but you forgot the most important one – jealousy between bosses and their own subordinates or the subordinates of others."

"But how does that manifest?" Jim asked.

"It manifests in many subtle ways. As a leader it's one of those things you must be alert to because you will only know it when you see or feel it. For instance, look for consistency in the message. When a person is being evaluated, is what is being said about them consistent? What about the past year's feedback? If the person was a star in past years under one boss and now is a loser under another boss, was it the person or the boss? Just a question to consider."

"Come on Ted!" Jim said, putting the pen down. "That is too subjective and not concrete enough. You need to do better than that if you want me to buy into this 'corporate jealousy' idea."

"Okay Jim, let's go to the video archives. This time, you will not only be able to hear and see what was said and done at the meeting, but I'll even let you hear the unspoken thoughts people had at the time."

Immediately, the three dimensional image of a past performance appraisal meeting was playing out before Jim's eyes. He recognized the meeting. It had taken place three years earlier, and he had been there. One of his colleagues, Terri, was presenting one of her people, and she was giving him a glowing review. She said he was achieving excellent results, was a strong team player, and was someone she thought should be moved up quickly. Jim could hear the words she was speaking, but could also hear the thoughts he himself was having while she spoke:

"This guy comes in here with no background in our business, and within two years he has moved up from an engineer to a manager. And now she wants to promote him to associate director? It took me eight years of working my ass off to make associate director and she wants him to get there in two. No way!"

"Oh my, Jim," Ted said, shaking his head in mock disappointment. "Did you really think that? Wow. Good thing you didn't say it out loud, huh? Too bad you acted on it, though."

Jim knew exactly what Ted meant.

The video continued. "Terri, do you really think that Peter is that good?" Mike asked. Jim remembered being glad Mike had challenged her so he didn't have to. "I mean," Mike continued, "he's only been here for a short time, and we can't really be sure that he's as good as you say he is."

"Well Mike, here's how I see it: Peter came to us with an incredible amount of experience from CC&A. When I hired him, I was impressed with his background – both practical experiences and results-wise – and also with his leadership qualities and maturity. I'm not only looking at what he has done for us in the past two years, but also what he can contribute to the company moving forward."

"Oh please!" Jim had thought to himself. "Go get her, Mike…"

"So you didn't want to do the dirty work, did you Jim?" Ted asked confrontationally. "You were glad that Mike was handling it for you, weren't you? In fact, you and Mike had sort of talked about this beforehand, correct?"

Jim was ashamed to admit it, but he and Mike had in fact discussed Peter before the meeting. They both knew that Terri would come in pushing strong for Peter to get promoted, and they did not feel it was appropriate. After all, it had taken both of them much longer than two years to reach that organizational level. And how would they justify it to their subordinates who also had been there longer than Peter?

The video played on. "Look Terri," Mike continued, "I'm not saying that Peter is not a good guy. In fact, I like him very much, but…"

"Freeze video," Ted called out. "So what's about to happen here, Jimmy?"

Jim knew that Peter was about to get thrown under the bus. Ted did not wait for his answer. He knew Jim got the point.

"Continue video," Ted ordered.

"I do have a few concerns about his knowledge of our business. I just think we need to give him a few more years of seasoning here at ITA. After all, we are not CC&A. We're in a different business. Jim, what do you think?"

"Terri, I guess I agree with Mike. Maybe we should let him develop another year or two."

"Seen enough?" Ted asked, bringing Jim back into the present with a jolt.

"Yeah," Jim said, sighing dejectedly.

"Where's Peter now?" Ted asked, adding salt to the already gaping wound.

"He's the VP of Operations at Bentley Corp."

"Really? Wait a second, isn't Bentley Corp your biggest competitor? And just how is Bentley doing these days?" Ted asked.

"They are coming on very strong, and actually giving us a bit of a hard time in the market place," Jim admitted.

"Peter was more than ready. In fact, Peter was better prepared than most of the people who were in the room judging him that day," Ted said, his voice tinged with anger. "The problem was that some people in that room only wanted to see what they wanted to see. The two years that Peter had spent at ITA were just the tip of his experience. When he was hired in this company, he could have walked in at the manager or director level. He was that good."

Jim sighed and rubbed his temples with both hands.

Ted softened his stance. "Don't feel too bad, Jimbo. This kind of thing happens every day in those kinds of meetings, unless the leader is alert enough to ensure that the process is not sabotaged by idiocy like you just witnessed. You see, sometimes rather than 'talent scope,' we should call these meetings 'style scope.' If we like the person or their style, then they must be good, but if we don't like them or if their style is different than our own or what we think it should be, we push them under the bus."

"I think I've got it. Talent that gets results is more important than style that looks or sounds good."

"Always! Bottom line, Jimmy, is that people audit processes are biased, because the people participating in the process are biased."

"So what can we do about it?" Jim asked, reaching for the pen. He was now convinced that Ted's concept was valid after seeing evidence of his own bad behavior in that meeting three years earlier.

"First, *check your own biases and make sure you focus on the facts*. Next, *don't tolerate comments by others that are not based on fact, or are based on hearsay*. Third, *ensure that the standards of measure are the appropriate ones – the ones that are best for the business – and are not based solely on the experiences of individual career tracks*."

"That's it?" Jim had hoped for more.

"What more do you want? It's about people dealing fairly with people. It's about you as the leader making sure that people are evaluated on a fair playing field, and remembering that it's not a popularity contest. It's not about who plays golf best or what football team they happen to cheer for."

"So, none of this 'he's a good guy' stuff," Jim volunteered.

"Oh boy, that one usually makes me go through the ceiling!" Ted said, waving both hands in the air. "How often do you hear someone say 'he's a good guy,' when describing someone during a succession planning meeting, or when trying to justify hiring them, promoting them, or giving them that 'special' assignment?"

Jim was about to answer, but Ted continued, "It's also not about what sports someone played in college, or who tells the best jokes at corporate functions. It's not about the brown-noser that everyone likes, and it certainly isn't about the person who has been hanging around the longest in queue waiting for a promotion."

"I may need a bit of help to make sure I remember all of that."

Just then, the phone rang. It was Dawn. "Hi Jim. I just wanted to let you know that we're ready for the meeting."

Ted looked at Jim and smiled. He knew Dawn would call at that very moment. Jim smiled back. "Dawn, I'm glad you called. I need to chat with you about a few things before the meeting. I need your help…"

Antidote to
Promotion-Induced Amnesia (PIA)
Dose #11
"Leaders must remember that there is corporate jealousy between peers, and between bosses and their subordinates."
Remember:

1. Check your own biases. Make sure you focus on the facts.
2. Do not tolerate comments by others that are not based on fact, or are based on hearsay.
3. Ensure that the standards of measure are the appropriate ones, and that they are applied uniformly across the individuals being rated.
4. Keep in mind to value talent and results more than individual style.

CHAPTER 6

"People Development is Job One"

Jim felt good on the way home that afternoon. He was satisfied that the succession planning meeting had gone better than any other he had ever attended.

"You did good today, Jimmy," Ted said, materializing in the passenger seat next to Jim.

"Yeah, that was a good meeting. I think we made excellent progress with our process."

"What do you think made it different than the others?"

"For starters, I think I set the right tone for the meeting. I made it clear that I wanted fact-based discussions, and that I expected everyone to have positive challenges for each other."

"What else?" Ted asked with a grin.

"Also, we made it a norm for the group that if there was going to be some negative remarks made, the person must be able to give concrete examples of the behavior that they were commenting on. That alone seemed to eliminate many of the 'hearsay' rumors and back-handed accusation-type of stuff."

Jim stopped himself and suddenly had a moment of doubt. Ted picked up on it immediately.

"You are wondering if they were just giving it lip service and just telling you what you wanted to hear, right?"

Jim sighed. "Do you think that's what went on?"

"What if it did? You can waste your time worrying about that, or you can capitalize on the momentum you started today."

"What do you mean?"

"Jimmy, today was all about people. People development, to be precise. I mean, why do we bother to do succession planning?"

"To ensure we have people ready to move into positions as we grow and change."

"Right! Unfortunately, these meetings often turn into posturing summits where folks try to place their golden children into advantageous positions, rather than discussing the needs of the organization, the individual's skills and abilities, and the development they need in order to progress and help the company meets its objectives."

"That's human nature, isn't it?" Jim asked.

"Maybe so, but your job as leader is to simply identify the right people, highlight their skills, identify their developmental areas, and figure out the best way to grow your talent so that you can grow your organization."

"Okay. I agree with that. But how do we put that to practice?"

"Glad you asked. Since you are driving, I'll even write these down for you." The magic pen and pad appeared suddenly and hovered between the two.

"First," Ted continued, "you must always remember that as a leader, people development is job one. That may sound cliché to you, but leaders have to be on constant watch over that process. If you don't focus on people development, no one else will.

"Got it."

"Second, don't make this into rocket science. Developing talent is not that hard. It just takes discipline. It's a simple process, but it must be followed."

"Let me take a whack at it," Jim said.

"Go."

"Step one is to *fairly evaluate individuals against a well- established and universally understood list of skill sets* that the organization thinks are the right qualities."

"Excellent start, Jim. Having a set of leadership qualities that define the standards and expectations for individuals to strive for is key."

Jim nodded in agreement. "Second, *specifically detail the individual's strengths and areas of improvement against these standards.*"

"Great. I'm glad you used the word 'detail' because that's where the process usually breaks down. "

"Absolutely. It was always frustrating to me to get feedback that I needed to improve in this area or that area, but often I would get no concrete examples to help me understand the feedback."

"Good. Keep going."

"Third, *identify a specific position or positions that the individual would be a good match for, and what the timing of such a move could be for them.*"

"And?"

"*Come up with two or three specific actions that the individual will take or things that they will do in order to help them grow and develop the areas of need.*"

"Really good. Why only two or three?" Ted asked.

"Because we will be doing formal succession planning meetings every six months, and if we are providing people real development opportunities or training, realistically, they can only do so much in that short period of time."

Ted was getting excited. "Yes!" he exclaimed. "Development is a long term process, so why try to change a person in only a few weeks, right? You've got to make it doable."

Jim continued. "Next step is to *communicate clearly with the individual to give them concrete, honest, and specific feedback, focusing not only on their areas for improvement, but highlighting their strengths.* We have to share our plan for them, and have a good understanding of what they want to do to determine whether their objectives and the company's are in alignment."

"You've been giving this some thought, haven't you?"

"Well, this happens to be an area that I think I've been pretty good at throughout my career." Ted knew it was true. This was a strength area for Jim; he was known industry-wide as a good people developer.

Antidote to
Promotion-Induced Amnesia (PIA)
Dose #12
"Leaders must remember that People Development is Job One."

1. Measure the person against established and universally understood criteria.
2. Establish a detailed list of strengths and areas of improvement.
3. Define next steps for the person.
4. Communicate with the person to gain alignment and crystallize the development plan.
5. Establish mentors who will help execute the development plan for the individual.
6. Own the development process.
7. Be a chance giver.

"Maryann mentioned that," Ted said absentmindedly.

"Maryann? How do you know her?"

Ted abruptly changed the subject. "Never mind. Now bring it home for me. What's missing in this whole people development cycle?"

Jim thought about it for a few seconds. "I'm not sure I've missed anything. I mean, like you said, it's not rocket science." Jim paused again and then began summarizing his list out loud. "You measure the person against the right criteria, you develop a detailed list of strengths and areas of improvement, you come up with possible next steps for the person, and you communicate with the person to gain alignment and crystallize the development plan. It seems pretty complete to me."

"Who owns it?" Ted asked casually.

Jim smiled. "Trick question."

"How's that?"

"Because if I say the individual does, you will remind me of how frustrating it was for me to hear that from my boss because I felt I could not really control it. If I say that the manager does, you will give me the speech about how each of us has to be responsible for our own development. And if I say both do, you probably will say that anything that is owned by more than one person is owned by no one. So it's a trick question."

"No trick. There is a correct answer."

Jim thought hard.

"I do," he announced, as if something had just been revealed to him. "I own it."

"That's right Mr. Givens. You own it. The leader owns people development in their organization. Period. If you don't insist that it happen, if you don't create a culture in which it can happen, if you don't kick people in the butt who don't do it, then it will not happen."

Jim was mesmerized. Ted's passion for the subject of people development was evident as he continued, "The leader who tries to delegate that responsibility to HR, or who would dare tell a high-potential person that their development is up to them, is not worth their weight in salt. People can't develop themselves. They need coaches, as well as specific and critical feedback given with the sole intent of helping them grow."

"People need assignments that will teach them new skills," Ted explained. "They need training opportunities. They need to be nurtured and cared for. They need to know that their leader believes they have a bright future, and they need to know what they can expect from the organization as they march toward that future. They need to clearly understand what the organization expects from them. They need to be linked with mentors who are held accountable by the leader for aiding their development process. And most importantly, they need…"

"Chances!" Jim said confidently.

That word hung in the air as they both contemplated its power.

"Chances," Jim repeated quietly.

"Think about it, Jimmy. What was the best development you ever got?"

"The stretch assignments, special and important projects, and positions that maybe I wasn't quite ready for," Jim said without hesitation.

"Yeah. Oh, you got great formal education along the way too, right? I mean, you had a chance to attend all the right classes to develop your business skills. You read lots of books? But nothing prepared you more than doing it. And you would not have done it had someone not given you…"

"A chance," Jim said, nodding his head.

"Even when others thought you were not the right guy for it, someone had to fight for you and put their neck on the line and say, 'you know, I think he really *is* the right person for the job.' One leader had to do that."

For the first time Jim realized that his success was not due exclusively to his ability and talent. Somebody, probably without him even knowing it, was always helping behind the scenes.

"People development can't occur without chances. And only leaders can give those," Ted concluded.

A few more quiet moments passed.

"Be a chance giver, kiddo. Remember to make people development Job One. Well, got to go. I'm late for my ballroom dancing class."

Jim's mouth dropped open. "You are taking ballroom dancing classes? You never cease to amaze me, old man."

Ted stood, twirled gracefully, winked and vanished.

"Hey wait… you never answered my question about Maryann!"

CHAPTER 7

Diversity Happens

The call came right in the middle of the board meeting. Jim's phone chimed out with the unique ringtone everyone had come to know as Marisol's.

"Hi babe. What's up?" he said, speaking as quietly as he could so as not to interrupt the meeting.

"Jim, my water broke and I'd like to get to the hospital now," Marisol said calmly.

"Okay. I'm on my way. I'll be there as fast as I can."

In a flash Jim was out the door and jogging to his car. He tried to control his breathing and his excitement.

As he sat in his car, he fumbled with the key. It took him three attempts to finally find the keyhole. He turned the key, fully expecting to hear his engine roar to life. Instead he heard nothing. Not a sound. Not even the click click click of a dead battery.

"You've got to be kidding me!" Jim said to himself.

He tried the key three more times. Not sure why, he angrily pumped the gas.

"Not now, please, not today," he mumbled. Then he stopped. Like a man who knows he has been had with a flawlessly executed practical joke, he leaned his head back on his seat and said, "Nice, Ted. Now can you please start my car so I can get home?"

"I had you going, didn't I!" Ted said, materializing in the passenger seat. The car immediately came to life and they were off.

———————

When Jim and Marisol arrived at the hospital, they were quickly escorted back to the labor and delivery ward. After filling out a few forms, having their insurance cards checked and copied, and exchanging not-too-many pleasantries with a nurse who was either pulling a double shift or was just naturally grumpy, Jim pushed Marisol's wheelchair into Room 203.

"Oh, this is nice," Marisol declared as she looked around the tastefully-decorated private delivery room that would be her home for the next forty-eight hours.

"Yeah, it's nice," Jim said, as he helped her onto the bed.

Just then, Nurse Kelly, a bubbly middle-aged woman, strode into the room. "Hi ya'll!" she said with a wide smile. "This is the big day huh? Well, we will take good care of you. My name is Kelly, and I want you to know you are in the best place in the world to have a baby sweetheart." From her accent, Jim guessed she was from the Deep South; Alabama, maybe.

"Now, Dad," Nurse Kelly said in a grandmotherly tone, "your job is to make sure this little lady here has everything she wants and to cater to her every whim, got it?"

"Absolutely. Yes ma'am," Jim said.

"Girl," Kelly continued, this time addressing Marisol, "you are lucky. Dr. McKenzie is on duty today. He is the best of the best."

"Dr. McKenzie?" Marisol said with a tinge of worry in her voice. "Isn't Dr. Moore here today?"

"Not today, hon. She was here last night until very late. But don't worry, sweetie, Dr. McKenzie is really good. I promise. You and your baby are in good hands."

There was a tap at the door and a lanky young man dressed in hospital scrubs poked is head into the room.

"Did I hear my name?" he said, stepping inside and extending his hand to Jim. "Hi, I'm Dr. McKenzie."

"Hello doctor, I'm Jim. This is my wife Marisol."

"Well hello, Marisol," he said, trying hard to speak with his best Spanish pronunciation. "That's a beautiful name. I'm guessing you are Hispanic?"

"Yes I am. It's nice to meet you, Dr. McKenzie."

"It's good to meet you, too. Well, let's take a look and see how we are doing."

After a quick examination and some more small talk from the doctor, he announced it would be a while before the baby was ready to make its entrance. He said he would check back later, gave Nurse Kelly some instructions and left as quickly as he had arrived.

──────────

The next few hours were uneventful, other than the normal labor pains and discomforts that Marisol suffered. Jim had called Marisol's mom and his mom, both of whom were in standby mode.

Every once in a while, Jim would replenish Marisol's cup of ice chips and would take his slow-moving wife for a short walk up and down the corridors.

"Atta boy!" Kelly said each time he walked by the nurse's station. "You look after your pretty girl."

Finally the big moment arrived, and the room that had once resembled a small hotel suite was quickly converted into what looked more like an operating room. Dr. McKenzie donned his gloves and a backward gown, the same kind that Jim now wore.

"Okay, Marisol, we are almost there," Dr. McKenzie promised after each painful push.

Jim did his best to encourage his wife, and did not complain when her fingernails dug deep into the palm of his hand with each agonizing contraction.

"One more Marisol. This is it! Come on. Bear down. Good job," Dr. McKenzie said as he positioned to pull the newborn into the world. "Okay. Don't push anymore. Relax."

Exhausted, Marisol fell back onto her pillow just as she heard her baby's first cry.

Jim, still holding his wife's hand, was transfixed on his new baby girl. Dr. McKenzie cradled her in one arm while he worked to clear her nasal passages and give one quick examination of the newborn. "That's great. She looks lovely. Congratulations Jim and Marisol, it's a girl."

Joyful tears rolled down both of Marisol's cheeks. Jim leaned down and gently kissed her on the forehead, his tears mixing with hers.

The next few minutes went by with lighting speed. Two nurses cared for the baby – one took measurements while the other took footprints.

"She's beautiful," one of the nurses said without looking up. "What's her name?"

"Her name is Michelle," Jim announced proudly.

"That's a beautiful name, Jim," Dr. McKenzie said as he stopped at the bassinet to take one last listen to Michelle's heartbeat with his stethoscope. "Sounds steady and strong. She is perfect." Just then Michelle grabbed the stethoscope and tried to put it in her mouth.

"How about that?" the doctor said. "Maybe she wants to be a nurse?"

One of the nurses rolled her eyes back and shot back, "Maybe she wants to be a *doctor*! Oh wait, she looks too smart for that!"

"Ha, ha, very funny, Jeanie," the doctor said, realizing that he had just made yet another chauvinistic comment. He had been chastised by several of the nurses on the ward for similar remarks over the years.

"I know, girls are just as good as boys. I got it, I got it," he said sincerely, with a broad smile. "I'm learning, you know, but old habits are hard to break. I mean, it's not my fault. It's the way I was brought up. Ain't that right, Jim? Help me out here, man – you're my only hope!"

"Uh, well, I think I'd better stay out of this one," Jim said.

"Smart man," one of the nurses said. "See, Dr. McKenzie? Not all guys think the same way."

Two hours had passed since everyone had left the delivery room. Marisol was in a deep sleep. She was exhausted, but her face had a peaceful smile on it. Baby Michelle was also sleeping serenely, lovingly tucked into the bassinet next to the bed.

Jim sat quietly in the comfortable chair beside them, and his gaze moved from his wife's face to his newborn daughter. Suddenly he realized that the hospital was going to make him take that baby home! She was now his responsibility. In a flash, the world he knew changed. His priorities were redefined then and there.

"She's beautiful, kiddo," Ted said softly from the corner of the room.

"Oh, hey, Ted. Thanks," Jim said proudly.

"What are you thinking about?"

"How lucky I am," Jim answered, unable to take his gaze from Michelle. "And how suddenly, all I can think about is what I need to do to make sure she grows up healthy and happy."

"And?" Ted asked, knowing that there was more on Jim's mind.

"And, wanting her to grow up in a world where she has the same opportunities as anyone else to do whatever she wants, to achieve whatever she sets her mind to, and to not have to put up with some of the stuff that I know Marisol has had to deal with."

Ted sat quietly. This was a moment of enlightenment for Jim, and one he needed no coaching to attain.

Jim was amazed at how much he already loved having a little girl. But from the moment months earlier when a sonogram revealed that Marisol was carrying a girl, he had become increasingly aware of the disparate way women were considered and treated in his company. He thought of the jokes he had heard about "girls" recently. He recalled "guy talk" over beers about some of the women who worked at ITA.

Jim considered what his own thoughts had been about women's roles in the workplace. He remembered discussions about whether promoting a woman was a good idea, since it was likely she would want to have a baby or two and would take maternity leave. He felt guilty for his thoughts and feelings when, recently, a woman on his team announced she needed to leave an important meeting early to pick up her child from daycare because her husband was working late that day.

Jim even remembered the anger he felt when that same woman called in on day two of the same critical meeting to say she would have to work from home. She had to care for her child, who had a bad cold and could not go to daycare.

Ted smiled, satisfied that this was going to lead to a good place for Jim — and for the people on his team.

Just then Marisol's eyes fluttered open and she squinted, looking toward the baby's bassinette. She smiled and closed her eyes again, quickly fading back to sleep with a whispered, "I love you." At first Jim wasn't sure if she meant him or the baby. Then he realized that she meant both.

"She's been through so much," Ted said, breaking the silence.

"Yeah. She's tired. I guess having a baby is as tough as they say it is."

"Oh yeah, that too," Ted replied. "But I was referring to where she came from, and how much she has achieved in her life."

"Yeah, she really has," Jim said softly. Suddenly, Marisol's life came into sharper focus for him. The daughter of immigrant parents, she spoke no English when she first arrived in America. She overcame great bias — both as a woman and as a Hispanic in a community with little diversity — to grow into the fine woman she had become. In Jim's eyes, Marisol could do it all. Yet he recalled the many nights when she came home irritated about something sexist that had happened to her in the office.

"I don't want Michelle to have to deal with the same things women do now," Jim said in a whisper.

Breakthrough!

"Diversity has just become personal for you," Ted proclaimed.

Jim nodded at Ted with understanding in his eyes.

Diversity was not a foreign concept for Jim. He'd heard about it for years in Corporate America. ITA had a diversity policy, and once in a while there was even a conversation or two on the topic at the senior levels of the organization. They usually took place during performance reviews and succession planning. Besides, Jim had married a Hispanic woman, and he had been to enough family gatherings to know there were stark differences between his background and hers.

"You know, kiddo," Ted said, "there are at least two reasons to give a damn about diversity. First, it's the right thing to do. Everyone deserves an equal opportunity to achieve whatever level of success they want to work toward in life. Second, it's the only smart way to run a business. The leader who refuses to create a diverse workplace environment or who doesn't leverage the power of the team's diversity dooms the organization to be less effective."

Jim considered Ted's words seriously. "It's not just about gender, is it?"

"Nope. But once you get that one, the other dimensions of diversity become clear."

"Tonight," Ted continued, "enjoy your daughter's birth and get some rest. Tomorrow, we begin the work of creating a culture of inclusion at ITA."

Three nights later, Jim was up for the 2 a.m. feeding. He was wide awake, so he headed to his study.

Ted's words had stayed with him the past few days.

"Dimensions of diversity?" he thought to himself.

"Jim, differences come in many flavors." Jim was only slightly startled by Ted's voice as it came from the comfortable chair on the other side of his desk. "Race and gender are just the ones that everyone thinks about first."

"I got you. You mean things like sexual orientation, religious affiliations, and things like that?"

"Yes, those and many more. There's educational background, military service, mental and physical abilities, social and economic status… I mean, we can keep going."

"How about style – you know, like communication style primarily? Or even family status? Married, divorced, single?"

"Absolutely," Ted said. "It's amazing how many ways we work to find differences between people and how we act based upon them, often without even recognizing it."

"Too bad we don't spend more time looking for and building on our similarities instead," Jim added. "Imagine the power we could harness if we did that!"

Ted smiled. "Yes indeed, imagine that! What if you could create a culture in your organization where that is exactly what happens. What might that be like?"

"Powerful. Effective. Competitive. Hard to beat!"

"Yes, yes, yes, and yes!"

"So it really is about maximizing the power of diversity in our workforce to create a culture of inclusion and to leverage our resources to drive business results?"

Jim had just recited ITA's diversity policy.

"Funny thing is most 'leaders' can recite the company diversity policy like you just did. But until a couple of days ago, how much have you really thought about it? How much have you really considered it as part of your daily routine as a leader? How much did you really believe it?"

"Truthfully? Not much."

"Jimbo, a leader never ever ever ever forgets about diversity, and always looks for ways to ensure that he or she is leveraging that diversity to drive dramatic results."

"Ted, the problem is that people don't always understand the 'why.' Why should they care? I mean, most people – me included – don't think they have 'diversity issues.' You know what I mean?"

"I understand exactly what you mean. Few people get it. Even fewer people think they have issues. Yet no one argues with the evidence and data that, for example, people of color are not promoted as often as their white counterparts. No one argues that even in the 21st Century, women are generally paid less for the same work as men in Corporate America. And no one argues that people of color and women leave organizations in larger percentages than their counterparts."

"Why is that?" Jim asked.

"You mean the last one? Why they leave in greater numbers?"

"Yeah, why is that?"

"The reasons are many, but let me give you just a few. Better opportunities elsewhere, for example. Some other company acknowledged their skill sets and was willing to offer them a position at a higher level now rather than later, and because someone showed them that they are important and that they matter."

"Hold on," Jim complained. "Those reasons have nothing to do with whether you are a man or a woman, black or white. Anyone would leave for those reasons."

Ted smiled. "You are absolutely right, Mr. Givens. But answer me this, oh Great Leadership Wizard, why then is it that people of color and women have the highest turnover rates? I mean, if you would leave for the same reasons as they would, why are they leaving more often?"

Jim carefully contemplated the question.

"So, do we have issues or not?" Ted asked.

"We do. I get it. But how do I make anyone care?"

"That's the right question, Jimmy boy. The answer is as simple as this:

like anything else in business, you must create a strong business case and a compelling business reason to do something about it. It's about global competitiveness."

Without notice the magic pen hovered before Jim's eyes, and he instinctively reached for it.

"I'm ready," Jim announced, expecting a lesson.

"Write these down. Number one: *create a business case for diversity.* Two, *model the behaviors and check your own biases.* Three, *educate everyone in the organization.* Four, *recruit for diversity.* Five, *check promotion slates.* Six, *check and challenge behaviors,* and seven, *recognize and reward those who model inclusive behaviors.*"

Jim wrote feverishly, trying to keep up with Ted. "Easier said than done," he said.

"That, my boy, is why you get paid the big bucks. Ignore this like most leaders do, and you are missing one of the most important elements in driving innovation in your company."

Antidote to
Promotion-Induced Amnesia (PIA)
Dose #13

**"Leaders must never forget about
diversity, and always look for ways to
make sure it (diversity) is leveraged to
drive dramatic results."**

Remember to:

1. Create a strong business case for diversity
   in the organization.
2. Model the behaviors and check your own
   biases.
3. Educate everyone in the organization.
4. Recruit for diversity.
5. Check promotion slates.
6. Check and challenge behaviors.
7. Recognize and reward those who model
   inclusive behaviors.

CHAPTER 8

Lead, follow or get out of the way

It had been three weeks since Jim's new baby girl had come home, and at Marisol's urging, he was headed back to work. He had truly enjoyed the last few weeks with the two most important ladies in his life. He also found time to reflect on everything that he and Ted had been talking about over the past several months.

Jim knew he had a lot of work to do to affect enduring organizational change. He wanted to create a culture that drove ITA toward becoming a more empowered, diverse, nimble, innovative, effective, and fun place to be. The past few weeks had offered him the chance to recharge his batteries, and he was ready for the challenge.

As soon as he stepped through the glass doors of ITA's entrance, Jim was greeted with a huge smile from BJ.

"Welcome back Jim!" she said enthusiastically, jumping to her feet and running around the reception counter to give him a big hug.

Jim returned the smile. "Thank you, BJ. It's good to be back. How have things been around here?"

"Oh, just fine, fine. You know, some good days, some bad days, and most of the time, people just living their lives, going about their business."

BJ was full of Southern charm, and was a woman who probably knew more about what was going on in the company than anyone.

"Well, you will have to tell me all the latest, okay?" Jim said. "I'll take you to lunch sometime this week so we can catch up. Sounds good?"

"Okie dokie. How's the baby, and Marisol?"

"Fine, thanks for asking," Jim said as he began to walk toward the stairs. "Well, I'd better get upstairs and jump back in, I guess."

"You have a good day, and welcome back."

Getting to his office was a challenge – albeit a pleasant one. He was stopped at least a dozen times by folks who were genuinely happy to see him, and who wanted to know all about the baby.

The first person he ran into on the stairs was Henry Birdman. Henry was a long time employee of ITA, and had worked his entire career in manufacturing.

"Hey Jim, welcome back! How are things? I mean, you know, the baby?"

"Thanks, Henry. It's good to be back. Baby is doing great."

"You probably have stayed pretty connected with the latest happenings around here, huh?"

"Actually, not really. I did my best to disconnect for the last couple of weeks and just focus on my family." Somehow Jim knew that Henry was about to give him a bird's eye view of some current critical issue within the plant. It's not that Henry was a bad guy or a gossip, but he always seemed to be at arms length distance from the issue; never blocking solutions, but never offering them either.

A few moments later, Mary Sayer came strolling down the stairs and joined Jim and Henry.

After the usual pleasantries, Mary was fully engaged in the conversation along with Henry, adding her own flavor to the story. Jim worked hard not to roll his eyes as Mary spoke. She sometimes had difficulty keeping her commentary positive.

Jim did his best to move on gracefully, saying, "Well, it's so good to catch up, but I really need to get in that office and start tackling my inbox."

He took only about fourteen steps before running into Keith Soap. Keith managed to compress every bit of the last three week's excitement into an entertaining four-minute monologue with all the drama of a Hollywood script. *He was entertaining, if nothing else,* Jim thought.

Finally, Jim was almost at his office door. He passed the kitchenette where a few folks were gathered for their Monday morning ritual.

"Hey Jim! Welcome back!" Penny Quarter and Brian Back said in unison.

"Hi guys. Thanks, it's good to be back. How's the coffee today?"

"Excellent. Let me pour you a cup," Brian said.

Penny, without skipping a beat, continued what she had been telling Brian before Jim came in. It took Jim only as long as he needed to pour a bit of cream and two sugars into his coffee to piece together the points Penny was making. It also took him only that long to realize how easy it was for folks to second guess decisions made or actions taken by others the previous week.

"I tell you what, that's surely not what I would have done," Brian concluded when Penny stopped to take a breath.

Jim nodded thanks for the coffee and quickly slipped into his office, but before he could sit behind his desk, he heard Ted's unmistakable voice.

"Are you sure you're glad to be back to some of this?"

"Oh, yeah. I'm a man on a mission. We've got some work to do, right?"

Ted smiled and said, "Yes, especially with folks like Henry 'Corporate Bird Watcher' Birdman, Mary Sayer, or more accurately Mary 'Nay-Sayer', Keith Soap-Opera, and Penny and Brian 'Monday Morning Quarterback'."

Jim laughed out loud at Ted's characterization of his team members. "Oh, they are harmless," he said.

"Oh, no they are not," Ted said, shaking his head. "School's in session, buddy boy. Grab your pen and take some notes."

Jim complied without complaint.

"Look Jimmy my boy, as a leader, you have only three choices: lead, follow, or get out of the way. Let's start with those that need to get out the way; or better said, those that the leader needs to make sure get out the way of progress."

"There are five types of individuals that get in the way: Corporate Birdwatchers, Naysayers and Critics, Soap Opera Players, Easter and Christmas Churchgoers, and not to be outdone, the Monday Morning Quarterbacks."

Jim was amused with the names. "I can't wait to hear this!"

"Simple, my boy. Let's start with the birdwatchers. What do we know about birdwatchers?" Ted asked.

"Generally, they walk quietly through the woods with large binoculars in hand looking for rare birds, right?"

"I guess that's right. A few things are sure though. They can see every detail with those lenses, can't they? Every flaw, every feather, all the colors. They take notes and make observations, but they don't disturb anything. In fact, their goal is to be completely unnoticed by the birds."

"That's right," Jim agreed.

"Well, Corporate Birdwatchers are individuals who stay near the action but never get in the game. They don't complain about much; they don't block actions. They just observe with binoculars from a safe distance, never taking a risk and never making any waves. Can you think of people like that?"

"Sure I can," Jim said without hesitation.

Ted continued, saying, "Well, the problem is that what we need are individuals who are actively involved in solving problems or coming up with creative solutions or innovative products. What we *don't* need are folks who can see all the faults through their binoculars, but are unwilling to engage in driving change and creating the future. If you have some Corporate Birdwatchers, get rid of them."

Jim was writing as quickly as he could.

"Not much to say about Naysayers and Critics right? I mean those folks are easy to identify. But left unchecked, they can poison others with their negative thinking. On the other hand, if you can turn them into Committed Critics, then maybe you can have a valuable member of the team."

"A Committed Critic?" Jim asked.

"You have not done all your required reading, have you?" Ted asked.

"I am a bit behind on a few items," Jim admitted.

"Well, get on it boy! Finish reading *Breakthrough Thinking*. López, the author, is a nice enough guy – although he's not the sharpest tack in the bag if you know what I mean – but he got it right in that little gem of a book. He describes the Committed Critic as a person who is a tough critic on the team's approach, decision, and actions. In fact, this person makes it their job to poke holes in the strategies and tactics. But one thing they are is committed to the overall goals and objectives. They know what the team wants to accomplish and they are onboard with making it happen. That's a Committed Critic, not just a critic!"

"Got it," Jim said. "Makes sense. It's okay to have critics, just not ones who make it their life's objective to simply be critical and negative."

"Bingo! Then of course you have your Soap Opera Players. These are your drama kings and queens – folks who are not happy unless there is some crisis; often one that they helped to create out of something miniscule."

"Boy, that one makes a lot of sense to me," Jim volunteered without looking up from the magic notebook. "Why is it that some people need to live in constant soap opera mode?"

"I suppose it gives their life some sense of excitement," Ted concluded. "Think about it, what are the characteristics of a soap opera?"

"Well, let's see," Jim began, smiling as he spoke. "The story is always the same. One person cheating on another, somebody stealing from somebody else, a family feud, some medical crisis, mix in some romance and gossip about one character or the next, and you have the makings of a great soap opera."

"Yep, and it may make for great mindless television entertainment, but it has no place in our company," Ted said unequivocally. "Not only is the soap opera everything you said, but one thing is certain – it can be all consuming for the people around the Soap Opera Player. In fact, one soap opera actor can quickly rope a dozen others into their crisis-filled fantasy world – and then who has time to focus on the company's mission?"

The phone rang and Jim ignored it, letting it go to voice mail. "Go on," he said. "This is good stuff."

"Okay, let's move on to the Easter and Christmas Churchgoers," Ted said.

"Yeah, what's that about?" Jim asked with a chuckle.

"You know how there are some folks who only go to church on special occasions? They put on their best clothes, say all the right words and get all holy for one or two Sunday mornings each year. But the other fifty Sundays, they are nowhere near a church."

Jim laughed out loud as Ted continued, "Problem with these folks is that they are not consistent, they are not truly engaged. They only appear to be interested, but in reality, they couldn't care less."

"They also just take up space. I mean, you can hardly find a parking spot at church on those two holidays," Jim added.

"Amen, brother!" Ted said. "So in the corporate setting, these are the people who look good, sound good, use all the right industry lingo, and attend all the right meetings – especially the ones where they figure they might get some exposure to the senior executives."

"But when you need people to get down and dirty in the daily grind, they are nowhere to be found," Jim said, mostly to himself.

"Wow. That sounds like something I should have said," Ted remarked, meaning it as a compliment.

Jim smiled, but did not look up from the notebook.

Ted continued, "Finally, let's get to the most annoying type of all: the Monday Morning Quarterbacks. It just drives me nuts that people who were not in the game and in the heat of the battle on Sunday want to criticize long after the game is over."

"I would have done this, or I would have done that," he mocked, rolling his eyes. "Frankly, I have no time for people like that. My answer to them is always the same: *where were you when the action was happening?* If you're not in the game, you don't get to criticize those who were."

"I could not agree with you more!" Jim said enthusiastically.

"Monday morning quarterbacks are nothing more than spectators with attitudes," Ted continued. "They are kinda like the Corporate Birdwatchers because they play from the sidelines, watching the action from a distance and not engaged actively in getting to solutions. But they are quick to point out everything that's wrong with what is being proposed by those who are in the game."

"It's like the fan sitting in the bleachers yelling at an umpire for making what they think was a bad call, or screaming at a player for striking out after swinging at a bad pitch?" Jim volunteered.

"Exactly like that," Ted said pointing at Jim with his cigar. "Spectators with attitude! There's no place on a great team for that type of person."

Jim kept writing even after Ted was done talking. He did not want to miss anything.

"So, what can the leader do about these people? I mean, let's face it; there is a bit of all of these types in each of us, right? Who does not like to do a bit of Corporate Birdwatching, or live in a soap opera scene from time to time? Heck, I know I've been a Monday Morning Quarterback now and then. Can't just fire everyone."

"I hate to admit it Jimmy, but you are right about that. There probably is a bit of that in everyone, and you can't fire everybody. So as a leader, what can you do? You can manage these people and make sure that these styles and attitudes don't permeate everything they do and negatively influence others in the organization. As always, you must start by modeling the behaviors you expect, calling out the unwanted behaviors, and coaching those who are not playing according to the cultural norms you've set as the leader. If all that fails, then you have to get them out."

Jim nodded in agreement. "Not rocket science," he said.

"Nope. Just plain good old-fashioned leadership. Just so happens that many leaders forget to do it all too often. Bottom line is this: people generally have three choices, lead, follow, or get out of the way. What are you going to choose, my boy?"

"I choose to lead," Jim said confidently.

"Excellent. That choice includes clearing the way for others to follow; and that includes dealing with the people who just get in the way. Now, I've got to go. Got a big emergency to deal with. It seems Disney just promoted someone who makes Goofy seem like a genius."

With that, Ted vanished, leaving Jim feeling like he had his work cut out for him now that he was back.

Antidote to
Promotion-Induced Amnesia (PIA)
Dose #14
"Leaders must never forget to deal with the five non-effective personality styles in the organization."
Remember to deal with:
1. Corporate Birdwatchers
2. Naysayers and Critics
3. Soap Opera Players
4. Easter and Christmas Churchgoers
5. Monday Morning Quarterbacks

CHAPTER 9

Give A Little, Get A Lot

Some weeks had passed since Jim had last seen Ted, but he had been so busy that he hardly had time to notice.

It was Sunday morning, and the sun was shining brightly. Jim was glad that Marisol had convinced him to attend church services on Saturday evenings instead of Sunday mornings. She needed to sleep, and he really enjoyed having the quiet mornings in his study to catch up on some reading. If he was lucky, the baby would have her morning feeding and then go back to sleep for a couple more hours.

Jim made his way to the kitchen where the automatic coffee maker, which he had programmed the night before, had just finished brewing a fresh pot of Bustelo coffee. The aroma filled the air and brought a smile to Jim's face. He warmed some milk before pouring the hot coffee into the pot to make a perfect *café con leche*. He had learned long ago from his mother-in-law to never pour cold milk into coffee; not if you expect to have a good tasting cup of java, anyway. One and a half spoonfuls of Splenda and a few twirls with the spoon, and *voila*! The perfect cup of coffee. Jim was pleased with himself.

As he opened the front door to reach for his Sunday newspaper, he heard a hearty laugh coming from his home office. He recognized the sound immediately.

"Hey, you're back!" Jim said with a smile.

"Miss me, kid?" Ted mused without looking up from the computer screen.

"What are you doing?"

"Oh, just catching up on a bit of Internet browsing," Ted replied.

"Really? I didn't realize you guys used the Internet."

"Of course. Who do you think invented it, Al Gore?"

"What was so funny a moment ago?" Jim asked, leaning over Ted's shoulder.

"Oh, it's this Chester Elton and Company. These guys are hilarious," Ted said as he clicked through the web site.

"Those are the carrot guys, right?"

"Yep. Great insights on employee motivation and recognition. You know what I like most about what they have to say about the subject?"

"What's that?"

"They don't complicate it! It disturbs me how so many so-called consultant experts want to overcomplicate the simple act of recognizing employees. But what is even more alarming is how few leaders really understand the value of making sure that their followers are properly recognized," Ted said.

"Is it really that simple though?" Jim asked.

"You think it's difficult?"

"Well, I just think there's more to it than just saying 'atta boy' or 'well done'."

"There might be, but boy, those two are a great start!"

"I know, and I agree. I am not saying that it has to be complicated, but it has to be done right, and in a large organization it can be a bit complex," Jim explained. Ted did not respond because he knew where Jim was going with this argument, and it was precisely the destination he was hoping for.

"I mean, in our company I think we do a fairly good job of rewarding people. We have a formal rewards program in place. It was created with input from an employee's committee. I was a part of it, in fact."

"How's that been working out?" Ted asked with a slight smile.

"Not bad. I mean, it's not perfect. But I think overall, people like it. I don't think we use it often enough. Every year we budget money for recognition and every year there seems to be some money left over. But overall, it's used frequently. It's pretty simple to do, and anybody can submit someone for recognition. They just go into the computer and use the recognition web site in the system to nominate another employee for an award." Jim stopped for a moment and sipped his coffee as he sat down on the chair across from his desk, where Ted normally sat.

Ted looked at Jim and asked, "And?"

"And, I guess I am sitting here wondering why our employees don't seem as motivated as I'd like them to be."

"That, my boy, is the right question for a leader to be asking," Ted said as he clapped his hands together, making a noise that only Jim could hear. "Why do you think that is?"

"I guess I'd have to first think about what motivates employees in the first place. What motivates *me*?"

"Now you are on to something, Jimmy boy," Ted started, and Jim felt a lesson coming.

"I have three words for your consideration: *incentivizing, recognizing* and *rewarding*." Ted paused to give Jim the chance to absorb what he was saying. "What comes to mind?"

Jim was a quick learner, and he made an immediate connection between the words. "If I *incentivize* followers, they should perform well. If they perform well, I should *recognize* them, and if we achieve the desired result, I should *reward* them."

"Yes, yes, and yes!"

"We've been focusing on the rewards without really paying attention to the incentives and recognition," Jim concluded logically.

"Amazing! It's that simple! Most organizations and managers focus on rewarding. Give people a bonus, or buy them dinner, or maybe hand out some coupons for a car wash, or let them select from a brochure for anything from a set of kitchen knives to matching his-and-hers fake gold watches," Ted said without even taking one breath.

"The board just approved the brochure with the new gifts to be included for the rewards program next year," Jim said, dejected.

"There's nothing wrong with that, Jim," Ted said reassuringly. "Don't feel bad. That's a good thing. Reward programs are a good thing. Heck, what employee does not like to get free stuff? No, that's not the problem. The problem is that the stuff can't be given in isolation. Like you said before, there's more to it than that."

The magic pen and notebook materialized from thin air and hovered right in front of Jim's face. "I guess school's in?" he asked.

"Ding, ding," Ted replied as he pretended to ring a bell. "Now this is going to be a refresher class, because I am sure you already know this stuff. I mean, you read the *Carrot* books right? You even heard Chester's hilarious presentation when you folks invited him to speak at your annual meeting a few years ago."

"He was great!"

"No doubt. But it would drive him nuts to know that all the great stuff he talked about never actually got implemented or incorporated into the organizational culture. So let's try again. First things first. If you are going to motivate your employees, you are going to have to be motivated first."

"What?"

"What do you mean, what? If *you* are not motivated, how in the heck will you be able to motivate others? The secret here is that you have to be self-motivated as the leader. Your enthusiasm will be contagious. If you are up, only then can you get others up. So start by understanding what motivates you, and make sure that you are staying motivated." Ted stopped and looked at Jim.

"What?"

"Again with the what?" Ted asked with sarcasm. "I don't see you writing."

"Oh, yeah. Sorry." Jim put his coffee cup down and grabbed the pen and notebook.

Antidote to
Promotion-Induced Amnesia (PIA)
Dose #15
"Leaders must incentivize, recognize and reward their followers."

"Now, let's start with how to incentivize employees," Ted continued. "Start with setting clear standards. Everyone needs to understand what is important to their team, the organization, and to their own success."

"Information is power, right?" Jim added as he wrote.

"Exactly. And the more power you share with your employees, the more motivated they become. Second, set high standards for yourself and for them. A high bar to reach is a heck of an incentive."

"Appealing to everyone's sense of competition," Jim remarked.

"Right again. Good. Third, be specific about the team's objectives. Clarity in these goals is paramount if people are going to be able to align to them, fully engage themselves in them, and want to achieve each of them. Remember the old SMART goals?"

"Specific, Measurable, Achievable, Realistic, and Time bounded," Jim answered instinctively. He had learned about SMART goals many years earlier in a management class.

"Well done. Since everyone knows this so well, why is it that so few remember to apply it when establishing objectives? Well, in any case, let's get back to the subject at hand."

Antidote to
Promotion-Induced Amnesia (PIA)
Dose #16

To incentivize:
1. Set clear standards.
2. Set high standards for yourself and your followers.
3. Set SMART Objectives.

To Recognize:
1. Do it on the spot and often.
2. Talk about it with others all day.
3. Make it personal for the individual, but public knowledge for everyone else.

To Reward:
1. Balance rewards with the significance of the accomplishment.
2. Recognize team members fairly.
3. Never underestimate the power of a well-delivered public announcement about the result being recognized.

"Next, list the rewards that they will get for achieving the objectives, right?" Jim asked.

"Not even close. The rewards come last because, to be honest, they are not that important. You see, they may be different for different people. Money might motivate some, while a warm, handwritten thank you note may be exactly what another person might find most rewarding. You need to stop thinking of rewards as the recognition process. Many companies make that mistake. The recognition process is not captured in a website where one employee nominates another for an award, or where an employee goes to pick out their fifteen-year anniversary gift. The process of recognition goes on every day, live and in person. One on one. One manager to an employee, one leader to a team, one associate to the other."

Jim nodded in agreement. He liked what he was hearing from Ted.

"Keep in mind what you are hoping to accomplish. It's not just about motivating an employee for a short period of time; it's about keeping your entire organization motivated all the time."

"That's a pretty lofty goal."

"That's exactly why it takes great leadership. A motivated organization is an organization that can accomplish anything."

"Next comes recognition," Ted continued. "There's a right way to recognize, and there is a wrong way of doing it. To do it right, pay attention, and when you catch someone doing something right, recognize them on the spot. Then talk about their accomplishments with everyone you run into that day. The word will get around!"

"That's true. It's amazing how word travels through the team. Good or bad."

"The smart leader understands and uses that phenomenon to their advantage to send highly motivational messages by recognizing individuals. Next, make it personal for the individual, but public knowledge for everyone else."

"That's good stuff."

"Glad you like it. Finally on recognition, set an example for everyone else to follow. Expect your staff and the managers in the organization to do this daily. Talk about it in staff meetings and send out messages reminding them to do it. If you don't expect it, it will not happen. Set the example that will drive the culture. Eventually it will become part of the normal everyday way of doing things. That's one of the reasons I like the book *A*

Carrot a Day. It gives you simple daily reminders of things you can do and say to keep employees engaged and motivated."

"We gave every manager a copy of the book after Chester came to speak to us."

"Well, maybe it's time you dusted off your copy and had everyone else dig theirs out, too."

Jim sighed. He knew Ted was right.

"Okay, so we come to rewards. Rewards are nothing more than a way to make recognition tangible. The main reason rewards can't replace recognition is because rewards can encourage the wrong behaviors sometimes."

"I can see that. If you reward a team financially for achieving a given objective, say, for the operations team to reduce inventory, they might go after it so aggressively that they cause backorder and impact our sales team in the field."

"That sounds like the voice of experience speaking right there," Ted chuckled.

"Absolutely. We often have a problem with aligning team's objectives and many times we create competing priorities in the organization," Jim said with conviction.

Ted nodded, encouraging Jim to elaborate. Jim continued, "That became clear at our last annual company meeting when we gave a cash award to the inventory reduction team. They had done an impressive job of reducing SKU's by more than fifteen percent. The goal was ten percent. After the awards banquet, the VP of Sales went to my boss, who was the VP of Operations, to express his displeasure with the team having been rewarded for creating a huge customer service issue in the field that the sales representatives were still trying to sort out."

"And that story repeats over and over again, either with teams or individuals," Ted explained. "That is why creating the right incentives, along with the right measures and objectives, has to come first. That's followed by recognition of the right behaviors, and finally rewarding the result! The only thing left to discuss is how to reward the result."

"And that depends on many factors, right?"

"Yes, it does. It is important that appropriate levels of rewards accompany the result. Not everything deserves a huge cash bonus. Again, what's the purpose of having a recognition process?"

"To motivate the team," Jim said quickly.

"To motivate the team?"

"Oh, to keep the team motivated *long term*?" Jim asked.

"Right. Motivating the team for a day is not the end game. Some things to keep in mind on how to reward individuals and teams are: first, *make the rewards balanced with the significance of the accomplishment*. Second, *make sure to recognize the members of the team fairly*. Notice I did not say to recognize them the same, but rather fairly. This is the hard part – deciding what the appropriate level of recognition is for each member of the team, especially if there is money involved."

Ted paused just long enough to take a puff of his smokeless cigar before continuing. "Finally, *never ever, ever underestimate the power of a well-delivered public announcement about the result being recognized*. Know the facts about what the individual or team accomplished, speak to the facts, highlight examples of the behaviors exhibited that led to the great result, and how each member of the team contributed to the overall success. This is an opportunity to give folks credit for having come up with new ideas, for doing things in a breakthrough thinking way, and for creating lasting value for the organization."

Jim was getting motivated just listening to Ted.

"Long after the person has spent the bonus, they will remember the words spoken about them during the recognition ceremony. Do it right!" Ted finished with emphasis.

"That is probably the most significant thing that we can say about recognition," Jim said. "Because improperly delivered, no matter what the reward, the recognition will fall flat on its face if the leader presenting it does a lousy job of delivering it."

"That, sir, you can take to the bank." Ted agreed.

"Glad you decided to pop in today, Ted," Jim said sincerely.

"Oh, don't get all slobbery on me now. But I appreciate the sentiment."

"So, I was right. There is much more to recognition than first appears," Jim said proudly.

"Boy, you ain't kidding. And here's something else about it; if companies ever did the analysis to put a cost on what they lose by not paying attention to a culture of recognition, they would be shocked. The cost of retention alone is staggering. One of the main reasons people leave their job is simply because they did not feel valued and recognized! Incredible, don't you agree? They don't leave because they felt like they were not being paid well, or because they did not like the medical benefits or the working conditions, or even their job. Most leave simply because somebody, especially their bird-brain boss, forgot to say 'thank you' from time to time. Or because they felt invisible when they came up with a good idea. The leader who doesn't get this needs to be replaced."

"Guess you've seen this a few times?" Jim asked.

"Sadly, I see it all too often," Ted paused for a moment. "Hey, tell you what, as a parting gift for tonight, I'll give you a few more tips on rewards and recognition. Heck, you won't even have to write them down. I'll do it for you."

As he finished speaking, the pen and notebook immediately left Jim's hands and materialized in Ted's. "I think you'll enjoy these."

"I am going to get another cup of coffee while you do that."

"Bring me one. Real sugar, none of that Splenda substitute for me."

Antidote to
Promotion-Induced Amnesia (PIA)
Dose #17

Tips for Rewarding and Recognizing:

1. Give people credit for their ideas.
2. Write personal thank-you notes.
3. Walk around and give people pats on the back, accompanied by an informed and sincere 'thanks'.
4. Give someone time off to enjoy with their family.
5. Be sure you are sincere in your recognition. Forced or faked recognition will backfire.
6. Make sure to formally recognize efforts via announcements.
7. Send a letter to the employee's spouse or significant other thanking them for their support of your employee.
8. Be creative and spontaneous in the way you recognize.
9. Make recognition a daily habit.
10. Don't forget to recognize your boss when appropriate.

CHAPTER 10

Culture & Strategy: Perfect Together

Jim was sipping on his Coke Zero and reading through the agenda for the upcoming board meeting. The entire day would be dedicated to Strategy. He winced as he read the short biography of the consultant that would be facilitating the discussion that day. He'd seen her in action before and she was pretty good, but she was sometimes too detailed about following the process, even for Jim's taste.

The board had done a good job of outlining the major parts of the strategy for the following year. There seemed to be alignment on direction and the top six focus areas. Now, Jim thought to himself, if they could just agree on the primary objectives by each major functional area, they would have a shot at creating a synergy that would drive success.

"Why do strategies fail?" came Ted's thundering voice from his usual corner by the window in Jim's office.

Jim jumped slightly in his chair. He was rather accustomed to Ted popping in, but once in a while he was still startled.

"Jumpy this morning?"

"Can't you signal before just materializing out of thin air?" Jim complained.

"Wouldn't be half as much fun then," Ted said with his usual smirk. "So, what's the answer?"

"Lots of reasons. Too many objectives set. No clear alignment between all the key stakeholders. Ineffective communication of the strategy to all levels of the organization, to name just a couple."

"All good answers. But the hard truth is that many strategies fail simply because the leader can't get folks mobilized behind it," Ted said casually.

As he finished his statement, the magic pen fizzled out of nothingness and hovered just a foot in front of Jim's nose. The magic notebook crackled as it became visible on his desk.

"Write this down: *Leaders must never forget that in order to mobilize an organization toward achieving strategies and objectives, they must ensure that the organizational processes are aligned to the organizational culture*," Ted said quickly, barely giving Jim time to keep up.

Antidote to
Promotion-Induced Amnesia (PIA)
Dose #18
Leaders must never forget that to mobilize an organization toward achieving strategies and objectives, they must ensure that organizational processes are aligned to the organizational culture.

"But don't our processes really define our culture?"

"That sir, is the sad truth in so many cases," Ted acknowledged. "But think about it. Is that what you really want? You know why the government is so bureaucratic?"

"Because they have a form for everything; even to order new forms," Jim answered.

"Exactly," Ted said enthusiastically. "They have more defined processes than almost any other organization in the world. There is a procedure for everything. And what culture does that create?"

"One in which everyone follows every step by the book," Jim responded.

"Right. No 'intellectual doers' in that game. Remember 'intellectual doers' from *Breakthrough Thinking*?"

"Yep," Jim replied as he finished writing.

"Only doers in this case. Processes can, and often do, define culture. That's not what you want; quite the contrary, in fact. You want to define your culture and create processes that allow you to effectively use that culture to achieve your strategic objectives."

"Hold up!" Jim said waving his hands in the air. "We want to define our culture? Culture is what it is, right? I mean, it is how the organization behaves, and what it believes in. It's about how people act day in and day out."

"Absolutely," Ted agreed. "What one word describes everything you just said?"

Jim thought about it for a minute. "Values."

Ted smiled and nodded. "Values!" he exclaimed. "Organizational culture is created, changed, accepted, and effective when values match and support the vision of the company."

"So let's talk about values," Jim prompted.

"Yes. Let's talk. Value statements describe the behaviors and attitudes that are expected from everyone in the organization," Ted began. "That's different from a vision statement that defines where the organization is going or what it aspires to be. Instead, values are those simple yet profound ideals that help give the organization character and personality. Can you think of examples of values that you believe would create the right culture to drive the strategies the board is going after?"

"I can think of a few. Intellectual curiosity, entrepreneurship, speed-to-market, prudent risk taking, confidence, global thinking, flawless execution, sound ethics, valuing diversity, transparent communications."

"Okay, okay. You got the idea," Ted complained, although he was secretly proud of his pupil. "These kinds of words describe values and indicate the 'how' to behave in the organization. But know this; the list should be short and crisp. Carefully chosen words that will maximize their impact, and will send the right message as to what is expected."

"But who chooses them? They can't come from the board. They would just seem like the 'flavor of the month' type of initiative and corporate talk."

"Very good, kiddo," Ted said. "They must emerge through a process of enrollment. Sure, the leaders must set the tone and the example. But just because the leader says we are going to value transparent communications, doesn't mean that it becomes a value. Now, if the leader models that behavior consistently, then it emerges as a value."

Jim agreed. "Right, the leader can't just climb to the mountain top like Moses and come down with two tablets inscribed with the organizational values. This would be the time for democracy and involvement by all in the organization, as they help to define our value system."

"Don't stop now, Jimmy boy. You are on a roll."

"As the leader, I model the behaviors, and I guide and influence the process," Jim stated confidently.

"Well done. Remember, values drive culture, which ultimately will drive the strategies and the results. It is pointless to set strategies if the team's values, and therefore its culture, can't support them."

"And once values are understood, accepted, and lived every day, the culture emerges, and we must ensure that our processes and policies allow the culture to blossom," Jim concluded.

"And there it is! Brilliant in its simplicity, isn't it? It is profoundly stupid to define your processes first without giving thought to what your values are, and what you want your culture to be. Even in highly regulated industries where many of the policies and processes are impacted by external factors, it is important to develop processes that meet all the external requirements while not stifling the culture you want to create. It can be done!"

"So, are you suggesting that we need to revisit our processes and procedures and change them?" Jim asked, knowing the answer, but also knowing what that meant.

"Absolutely. As often as necessary, to ensure that they are not creating values you don't want in your organization."

"I was afraid you were going to say that."

"Now," Ted began, "let's talk about a few myths about organizational culture. There are many we can cover, but let's talk about the most important ones. Write this down: *Myths of Organizational Culture*. First, *it can't be measured so it can't be changed predictably.*"

Jim was writing as quickly as he could.

"Reality is," Ted explained, "that there are many good measurement tools available. They don't have to be complicated. The key to measuring culture is consistency in the use of the tool. Whether you choose to use a Connectivity Survey or some other survey tool, it does not really matter. The key is asking a few critical and important questions, doing it frequently enough to track progress and changes, and acting on the findings. We'll talk more about the type of questions to ask later."

Antidote to
Promotion-Induced Amnesia (PIA)
Dose #19
Myths About Culture
Leaders must remember not to fall for these traps:

1. Culture can't be measured so it can't be changed predictably.
2. Leaders communicate culture.
3. Culture does not impact company strategy, or vice versa.

Jim nodded indicating his understanding, so Ted continued. "Myth number two: *leaders communicate the culture.*"

As soon as Ted finished saying that, Jim looked up for a moment and said, "That's not true! Leaders behave the culture and thereby communicate it."

"Right. Myth number three: *culture does not impact company strategy or vice versa.* Well, we already spoke about that. These two things are in fact inextricably linked."

"Big word there, Ted!"

"Never mind the wise comments, Jimbo. Look, the company strategy defines what the company will do; its objectives, winning tactics, and desired outcomes. It sets the tone. Do you follow me?"

"Yes I do. For instance, a 'win at all costs' attitude will create a different culture from 'be number one in sales in our industry.' And if we state an objective to 'beat the competition,' that's very different than saying 'provide the best customer support.' They may both lead to the same outcome, but we will get there in very different ways," Jim said.

"Now you got it," Ted said. "No strategic objective written on any document stating 'we will value and recognize risk taking' will encourage prudent risk taking if the one who does take a risk and fails, is punished for it. So the leader must act in a way that is consistent with valuing risk taking. The leader's actions always speak louder than words."

"Okay. I got it. And that is all well and good, but let's get down to a few more specifics," Jim suggested, holding the magic pen in his hand.

"What do you think are the most important questions a leader must ask on organizational culture?" Ted asked.

Jim thought about it for a moment. Then he began to write in the book. He wrote three statements:

1. *What, why and who have we rewarded and recognized recently?*
2. *What do connectivity survey results say? What are we doing about it?*
3. *What behaviors are leaders modeling in the organization?*

Ted didn't even look at the notebook, but he knew what Jim had written. "Very good, my boy. Very good! Now, the next question is this: what are the most significant behaviors a leader must exhibit to impact culture?"

Again Jim gave it some thought, and began to write:

1. *Always tell the truth.*
2. *Speak clearly and transparently.*
3. *Act consistently, firmly and fairly.*
4. *Model organizational values.*
5. *Reward those who are modeling values.*
6. *Be decisive. Take prudent risks.*
7. *Admit mistakes. Learn from them. Move on.*

Ted was pleased with his student. He smiled. Jim finished writing and looked up at his teacher.

"What are you smiling about?" Jim asked Ted.

"I didn't give you the answers, did I? You knew them all along, like most of what we've talked about for the past many months. That's the amazing thing about 'the leader's lobotomy' and 'promotion-induced amnesia.' It can be avoided if leaders simply apply the things they already know!"

Jim smiled and nodded in agreement. He was pleased with himself.

Antidote to
Promotion-Induced Amnesia (PIA)
Dose #20

The most significant questions a leader can ask about culture are:

1. What, why, and who have we rewarded and recognized recently?
2. What do connectivity survey results say? What are we doing about it?
3. What behaviors are leaders modeling in the organization?

Antidote to
Promotion-Induced Amnesia (PIA)
Dose #21

The most significant behaviors a leader must exhibit to impact culture:

1. Always tell the truth.
2. Speak clearly and transparently.
3. Act consistently, firmly and fairly.
4. Model organizational values.
5. Reward those who are modeling values.
6. Be decisive. Take prudent risk.
7. Admit mistakes. Learn from them. Move on.

CHAPTER 11

L.E.G.A.C.Y.

One year later

Jim was sitting in his office enjoying an unusually quiet moment. Every once in a while when the weather was just right, Jim could watch the sunset from his desk. He especially liked watching the flickering lights that reflected off the glassy surface of the small lake on ITA's campus.

"Feeling pretty good about things, are you?" Ted asked quietly, trying not to startle Jim.

"Oh, hey Ted," Jim said with a broad smile. "Yeah, I'm feeling quite good about things."

"Well, you should be. You've done well this year. I am very proud of you," Ted said sincerely.

"Well, thank you, sir. A compliment from you? You feeling okay?"

"Oh shut up, smart alec," Ted snapped.

"There we go! That's the Ted I know and love!"

Jim said, returning his gaze out the window. "I just got back from the board meeting where we reviewed company performance and results for the past year. But I guess you already knew that, right?"

"Of course," Ted said casually. "The company is doing well, and your organization has had outstanding results in the past year. Well done."

"Thank you. I am very proud of my team," Jim said.

"Well, you had much to do with it, my boy."

"Not really."

Ted smiled. He nodded, pleased with himself and with Jim. He sat silently for awhile.

"I happen to have a fantastic team of dedicated people who make it look easy," Jim volunteered.

"Yes, they are all that. But, maybe, just maybe, you've had a little bit to do with it?"

Jim looked at Ted with a slight confident smile. Ted was pleased that Jim remained humble in his success.

Ted waited a few seconds before speaking. "Maybe it's taken a leader who engages them in a common vision, who communicates honestly, consistently and transparently, who cares for them personally, and who worries about their development and growth. What do you think, maybe it takes a leader who pays attention to organizational culture issues and recognizes their efforts and accomplishments?"

"Maybe it has taken a leader who has insisted on staying connected with his followers, and who has challenged their thinking," Ted continued. "And maybe it has taken a leader who dealt fairly and swiftly with performance issues, ensuring that those not contributing to the team's goals were dealt with."

"Yeah, maybe," Jim said, this time with a broad smile on his face. "Common sense stuff that anybody could do."

"And so we've come full circle. I seem to recall that is where we started way back when, isn't it? We started with the notion of leadership being all about common sense, and being applied daily."

"It's not rocket science. It's leadership!" they said in unison, laughing.

"It may be common sense, but there is nothing common about the leader who applies the leadership principles we've talked about over the past year or so," Ted said with conviction.

"I've been thinking about the question you left with me the last time we spoke," Jim said. "Do you remember…"

A knock on the door interrupted Jim.

"Hey, who you talking to?" Maryann asked, peeking her head into Jim's office.

Jim sat up quickly and glanced at Ted, who was still sitting three feet away from him. "Oh, no one. Just thinking out loud, I guess. Come on in. I thought everyone was gone at this late hour."

"We all should be, that's for sure," Maryann said as she made her way to the chair where Ted was sitting. For a moment, Jim thought Maryann would sit right on Ted's lap, but he was relieved when she reached for the other chair and pulled it up beside Ted's.

"So," Maryann began, looking at Jim. "How's our kid doing?"

Jim was nervous, although he didn't know why. After all, Ted was invisible to Maryann. "You mean my baby girl, Michelle? She's good. Growing like a weed," Jim said, shifting uncomfortably in his chair.

"She means you, Beavis," Ted growled.

"Huh?" Jim whispered, hoping Maryann would not hear him.

"She's not asking about you your baby," Ted said as he turned and looked directly at Maryann. "He's done quite well. Frankly, even better than I had expected," he said.

Maryann looked at Ted and smiled. "I knew he would," she said proudly.

"Well, you laid a strong foundation over the past few years, so all I really had to do was make sure he didn't forget the easy stuff."

Jim jumped to his feet.

"Whoa, whoa! Wait a minute! You can see him?" he asked Maryann with disbelief.

"She can see you?" he asked Ted.

"You guys know each other?" he asked both.

Ted and Maryann burst out laughing.

"Who do you think put in the request upstairs for me to be assigned as your CGA?" Ted asked with a chuckle.

Maryann looked fondly at Jim. "I knew Ted was the right angel for the job," she said. "Jim, I am so proud of the leader you have become over the past years. You have been modeling all the behaviors that make leaders and their organizations successful, and the results show!"

"I don't know what to say Maryann. I... I really appreciate everything you have done for me," he said humbly.

"And as for you," he said turning to Ted, "you have been a royal pain in my behind for the past year and a half."

"My pleasure. It's what I do," Ted said as he puffed on his smokeless cigar.

"Thank you," Jim said sincerely.

"Don't thank me too much yet. Your work isn't done. You are off to a great start, but the hard work is avoiding PIA in the long term."

"The key, Jim, is to stay focused on the basics of leadership day in and day out, and to not succumb to the symptoms of PIA," Maryann interjected. "Did you work on the last lesson yet?"

"We were just getting to that," Ted answered. "So, Jimbo, what about it?"

"You mean, my homework?"

"Legacy," Maryann volunteered. "One of the most powerful words in the English language. It's the only thing we take with us when we are gone. It amazes me how few people give thought to what they want their legacy to be."

"And even if they do give it some thought," Ted interjected, "they don't really consider how they want to go about building the legacy they want to leave."

"Jim," Maryann said with a motherly tone in her voice, "defining your legacy as a leader, and how you want to go about constructing it, is a very personal thing."

"I've been thinking about it a lot lately. I even came up with an acronym for it so I could remember it daily. And also so that I can make sure I am acting in ways consistent with the legacy I want to create as a leader," Jim said earnestly.

"Good! Let's hear it," Ted said.

"Here goes: L is for Lead and Love. E is for Educate, Evolve, and Empower. G is for Give and Grow. A is for Attitude. C is for Creating something of lasting worth. Y is for You. Because only you can determine what your legacy will be."

Jim had recited these from memory. He had clearly given it a great deal of thought. The three of them sat silently for awhile, thinking about what he had just said.

Finally, Jim spoke. "Here's my thinking on this: If you are going to create a legacy you and your family can be proud of, you have to first lead from the heart and love what you do. Otherwise, you will simply not be as effective as you should be as a leader."

Maryann and Ted looked at one another with satisfaction.

Jim continued, "Next, you must constantly evolve and learn. A leader must make education a priority. They must never stop learning. It is through learning that they empower themselves. And only an empowered leader can create an environment in which others can be empowered. We all know that an empowered workforce can't be beaten."

Ted raised an eyebrow at that last statement and thought to himself, *that's good! I'm going to have to remember that one and use it on my next pupil.*

> ## Antidote to
> ## Promotion-Induced Amnesia (PIA)
> ## Dose #22
> **Leaders must consider what they want their legacy to be, and act in ways consistent with that on a daily basis.**
> ☐ *L is for Lead and Love*
> ☐ *E is for Educate, Evolve and Empower*
> ☐ *G is for Give and Grow*
> ☐ *A is for Attitude*
> ☐ *C is for Create*
> ☐ *Y is for You*

"The 'G' was easy for me," Jim said. "It's simply to give. Give of yourself and you will grow. My dad always taught me that. The amazing thing is the more you give, the more you get. Next is A for attitude. It's one of the few things you get to choose on a daily basis. In fact, you can choose it many times throughout the day. Too many people choose the wrong one. I think it's important that the leader consider their attitude and demeanor. It sends a very loud message to those he or she leads, and it sets a pace and a tone for the whole organization. The leader's attitude has a huge impact on organizational culture!"

By now Maryann's pleasure was written all over her broad smile. Ted beamed like a proud papa as well.

Jim could tell that they both were enjoying hearing about L.E.G.A.C.Y. "The C is my favorite. Create something of lasting value. At the end of the day, that is the leader's primary reason for being. Too many leaders focus on the short term, or the financial rewards that can come with that short term thinking. Too many think that when they arrive at the top spot, it's their time to enjoy being the boss rather than their time to serve their followers. Too many worry about being popular rather than worrying about making the hard decisions that will serve the organizational greater good. And too many think it's about them rather than about those they lead."

"Amen brother! Maryann, we have ourselves a genuine philosopher here," Ted said.

"I wasn't trying to sound philosophical. I just wanted to make the point that leaders should worry first about creating a future that is better than the present. They should realize that their legacies will be directly linked to how they go about accomplishing that."

"Well said, my boy," Ted said.

"Finally the Y is for you. Only I can determine what my legacy will be. I choose my attitude, my actions, the path I will travel, and how I will lead. It's up to me."

Again the room fell silent.

Ted folded his arms across his chest and announced, "My work here is done."

Maryann turned to Ted. "Thank you for everything, my old friend."

Ted smiled at her and gave her a sharp military salute. "Always at your service, Ms. Maryann."

Ted looked tenderly at Jim. Jim had never seen him look that way, and he knew that he would not see Ted again.

"Be great, Jimmy boy."

And with that, Ted vanished.

THE BEGINNING

Epilogue

When my friend Anthony Lopez wrote the first edition of The Legacy Leader in 2003, he did it to keep a promise to his mom. While she was battling cancer, she challenged her son to publish his work. What could he say but 'yes mom'. Over the next year he got it done, and he was able to present his mother a signed and dedicated copy of the book six months before she passed away.

Tony selected the title of the book very carefully. In his view leadership is entirely about creating a legacy that each of us can be proud of. For him, it's personal. It's about creating a legacy his wife and daughters can be proud of. It's about creating a legacy that those who work with him over the years can be proud of. It's about creating a legacy his mom and dad can be proud of.

Over the decade, what began as promise kept became a journey of discovery. Tony has written five books and has created what we now know as the Legacy Leader Series of books including: The Legacy Leader – 1st and 2nd Editions, Breakthrough Thinking: The Legacy Leader's Role In Driving Innovation, The Leader's Lobotomy: The Legacy Leader Avoids Promotion Induced Amnesia, and The Leader In The Mirror: The Legacy Leader's Critical Self Assessment. Together they help describe the leadership journey, and provide a comprehensive view of what leadership is and what it is not. Most importantly, it provides all leaders willing to do the hard work, a road map that they can each use to aid in their personal leadership journey.

In the Legacy Leader Series, Tony takes us through the entire cycle of leadership, beginning with the fundamentals and mechanics of leadership. Building on these, we learn to apply them to lead our teams in achieving breakthrough results. The next phase of the journey is about reminding ourselves of lessons learned along the way, and making sure we don't repeat many of the mistakes we will undoubtedly make. Finally, in this latest installment in the Series, Tony causes us to take a hard look in the mirror and evaluate our performance as leaders. For those willing to be honest with themselves, this may be the toughest part of the journey.

In my personal leadership journey, I've experienced success and failures along the way. Through the years, I have read many leadership books – even some great ones. The Legacy Leader books are relevant, practical, entertaining, and impactful. The challenge to all of us who have the privilege of leading people is: are we willing to be emotionally intelligent and evolving leaders who are intellectual curious and excited to grow? If the answer to this question is yes, then these books will help. If we are mindful of the legacy we will create as leaders, and want to leave one that we can be proud of, then these books will be invaluable. Enjoy the journey.

Thomas J. Sullivan

President & Chief Executive Officer

Symmetry Medical Inc.

About the Author

Anthony López is the author of *The Legacy Leader: Leadership With a Purpose, Breakthrough Thinking: The Legacy Leader's Role in Driving Innovation* and *The Leader's Lobotomy: The Legacy Leader Avoids Promotion-Induced Amnesia.* He is also the author of two Christian books titled: *See You at the Wake: Healing Relationships Before It's Too Late* and *Jag: Christian Lessons From My Golden Retriever.* He is a popular motivational speaker, and is a recognized expert on leadership and management. Tony began his career as a US Air Force officer where he served as a flight test director and program manager. Tony later served as a human resources officer in the Air Force Reserves. He joined Johnson & Johnson in 1991 and held leadership positions in corporate engineering, manufacturing, marketing, communications, and general management. Later he was global vice president for marketing at ConMed. Tony is president of L&L Associates, a leadership and management consulting group he founded in 2000. He was also an adjunct professor at the Richard T. Dormer School of Business and Management Sciences at Indiana Purdue University. In 2009 Tony was named senior vice president and general manager for the respiratory business in CareFusion, based in San Diego, California. In 2011, he joined Ansell Healthcare as President of the Global Medical Business Unit. Tony holds a BS in electrical engineering, an MS in engineering management, and is a graduate of the Department of Defense Equal Opportunity Management Institute. You can contact Tony at: ablopez85@yahoo.com. For more information, please visit www.thelegacyleader.net.